WHEN
EDMONTON
Was Young

TONY CASHMAN

WHEN
EDMONTON
Was Young

THE UNIVERSITY
of ALBERTA PRESS

Published by

The University of Alberta Press

Ring House 2

Edmonton, Alberta, Canada T6G 2E1

Copyright © 2009 Tony Cashman

Library and Archives Canada Cataloguing in Publication

Cashman, Tony, 1923–

    When Edmonton was young / Tony Cashman.

Includes index.

ISBN 978-0-88864-511-1

    1. Edmonton (Alta.)—History—Anecdotes. 2. Edmonton (Alta.)—Biography.
I. Title.

FC3696.36.C373 2009   971.23'34   C2008-907139-5

All rights reserved.

First edition, second printing, 2010.

Printed and bound in Canada by Friesens, Altona, Manitoba.

Copyediting and Proofreading by Leah-Ann Lymer.

Indexing by Judy Dunlop.

The University of Alberta Press is committed to protecting our natural environment.
As part of our efforts, this book is printed on Enviro Paper: it contains
100% post-consumer recycled fibres and is acid- and chlorine-free.

The University of Alberta Press gratefully acknowledges the support received for its
publishing program from The Canada Council for the Arts. The University of Alberta
Press also gratefully acknowledges the financial support of the Government of Canada
through the Book Publishing Industry Development Program (BPIDP) and from the
Alberta Foundation for the Arts for its publishing activities.

Contents

Foreword

TONY CASHMAN IS A TELLER OF STORIES.

To confirm this "historically accurate" fact, one only has to sit a while with this gentle man. I have had the pleasure of sharing many a lunchtime visit with Tony in recent years. During these visits, Tony has shared with me about being "born in Edmonton in 1923, in time to grow up listening to the stories of two families attracted to the booming young city of 1906. These tales, and those of friends, showed a lively, companionable place where fun things happened!"

I find it remarkable to be writing a foreword for *When Edmonton Was Young* fifty-three years after Tony's first book was published. *The Edmonton Story* grew out of a series of radio programs on CJCA, in which Tony gave a ten-minute view of earlier Edmonton through cheerful tales of the kind he had listened to while growing up, but that no one had thought important enough to write down. From 1951 to 1961, there were 723 programs, all sponsored by Gainer's packing plant. *The Edmonton Story* had three sequels and led to a number of institutions commissioning Tony to tell their histories: *Heritage of Service* recalled the history of nursing in Alberta for the Alberta Association of Registered Nurses; *Singing Wires* told the story of the telephone in the province for Alberta Government Telephones. Others followed for such varied institutions as the Alberta Motor Association, Edmonton's Catholic Schools, Edmonton Exhibition Association, University of Alberta Hospital, and then, in 2002, Tony wrote *Gateway to the North* for the Edmonton Regional Airports Authority. The stories led to a scenario for a ballet, *Miette's Wedding*

(1967) and more recently to historical plays at the Edmonton Fringe Theatre Festival, of which there have been eight. Tony's work resumé included being news reporter at CJCA, program director at CKUA, and historian and museum curator for Alberta Government Telephones.

When Edmonton Was Young continues Tony Cashman's traditional interesting and amusing delivery of tales that highlight touching everyday moments in Edmonton's history. The book provides a delightful range of stories about Edmonton personalities from Jimmy Smith, the Mayor of the South Side, to Reg Lister, caretaker of student accommodations during the University of Alberta's early days, to Mrs. Mary Rennie of the Scots boarding house. It also tells tales about visitors like Lady Aberdeen, wife of the governor general in the 1890s.

My favourite *When Edmonton Was Young* story is about "The Curé of Partoutville," as it includes a little gem related to an Edmontonian's story that still needs to be documented in full, and that is the story of Tony Cashman himself. This is the story of Father Joseph Aldric Normandeau, who was a friend of Tony's grandfather, Mr. J.J. Cashman, business manager of the federal penitentiary that was located east of downtown from Jasper Avenue up to 111 Avenue. Following this story, Tony includes a personal postscript about his grandfather and the family home that was located at 10243–124 Street.

Over our lunches, Tony has shared stories about the many generations of his family—from his grandparents to his parents to his almost twin brother, John (there are a couple of years between them, but they have a striking similarity!), to his much loved wife Veva to his three sons Hal, Bernard, and Paul, to a beautiful daughter-in-law, Laurel, right down to a very talented granddaughter, Helen, who made her grandfather very proud when she helped to open his most recent Fringe play by dancing a lovely Irish reel! He has taken me on a "words and voice" journey that included a brief few years as a child living along the west coast of the United States, his family's return to Edmonton, his education at Grandin and St. Joseph's High School, WWII service as an Air Force navigator in England and university studies at Notre Dame in South Bend, Indiana.

In one conversation, Tony described a favourite personal experience in which he and Veva put on a program at Jasper Park Lodge for Elderhostel based on his books *An Illustrated History of Western Canada* (1971) and *A Picture History of Alberta* (1980). It was a six-hour multimedia production, incorporating video and audio clips, photographic slides and audience participation, with Elderhostelers taking on the personalities of people in history. It played eleven idyllic weeks in Jasper in mid-winters of the 1990s. In the fall of 2008, the production was revived with great success on six Wednesday evenings at the Provincial Archives of Alberta.

Tony Cashman is indeed a kindred spirit in my desire to preserve Edmonton and Alberta's documentary heritage, and a good, good friend. He is passionate about this city and his audience is passionate about his message. Tony is a quintessential teller of Edmonton's story!

Leslie Latta-Guthrie
Executive Director & Provincial Archivist
Provincial Archives of Alberta
November 2008

THE

MAYOR

OF THE

South Side

THE MAYOR OF THE SOUTH SIDE was as canny a Scot as the land of misty glens ever exported to Canada. Though Strathcona accepted the name of its cross-river rival in the Amalgamation of 1912, it never surrendered its individuality, its view of life, or its pace, all of which were intact when people of the exploding city discovered the charm of Old Strathcona right in their midst. Through the 1920s and 1930s, Jimmy Smith was hailed as the Mayor of the South Side. The title was honorary, but unlike many such titles, it was earned. Jimmy earned it every day.

Jimmy Smith was a small man, never much bigger than he was in 1903, when he arrived in Strathcona at age eleven with his mother, two sisters, brother Jock the baker, and brother "Wee Duncan" the plumber, who played cornet in the town band.

The Smiths lived just below Saskatchewan Drive in the present Queen Elizabeth Park. Jimmy's mother, a gregarious lady, friend and accomplice of auctioneers, helped support the family. She would mingle with the crowd at sales, and when an important piece was put up for bids, she would shout the price that had been secretly suggested by her friend the auctioneer. In the event of a bidding war, Mrs. Smith would go to war on behalf of the auctioneer. Jimmy thought the world of his mother and treated her like a queen.

At age eleven, Jimmy figured he had enough education for a shrewd Scot to make his way in the world and got a job herding sheep for Gainer's packing plant. After a couple of years with the sheep, he graduated to horses, driving a team for Durrand's Transfer. When Durrand gave up the business, Jimmy took it over. When automobiles began to take over the streets, he went into the business with which he was long identified: he bought a Maxwell and hung a taxi sign on it. Though his fleet never increased beyond three, they were enough to cover the South Side during his two decades "in office."

While the mayors of Edmonton had to deal with boring stuff, Jimmy Smith dealt in fun and games, revolving around two storied institutions of which Jimmy was top man. He leased from the city of Edmonton the fabled South Side Covered Rink (about where the Yardbird Suite sits today), scene of fierce partisan hockey games and fancy dress balls. As well, as president of the South Edmonton Businessmen's Association, he ran the South Side Athletic Grounds (now part of the Harry Ainlay complex). He made sure there were enough pals at the annual dinner meeting of the association to keep him elected. "There's nothing I hate worse than a fixed meeting," he confided, "unless I fix it myself."

Jimmy spoke in little explosions. If you were to follow him along Whyte Avenue, you'd hear: "'Lo, Ed." "H'are'ya, Doc?" "'Lo, Harold." "H'are'ya, Mrs. Fisher?" He wore a vest that became a South Side institution. It matched neither coat nor trousers, and his shirt was always spilling out from under the vest. His face was the colour red, for which there were three reasons. He inherited his complexion. He was outdoors most of the time. And then there was the third reason: his face would glow with pleasure when he presided at some event where people were having fun.

Jimmy might have become a wealthy man if he'd devoted as much energy to raising money for himself as he did to raising it for community entertainment. He was invariably hard up. When someone came to the taxi office trying to collect a bill, he could easily leave with five dollars less than he took in—a contribution to the South Side Athletic Club junior hockey team.

In 1937 the team and the community lost their beloved Covered Rink. The building had to come down before the roof came down on a crowd. It was a loss, but by no means a total loss. The remains were hauled to the Athletic

Grounds and resurrected as a horse barn—which Jimmy and the boys eventually sold to the provincial government for two thousand dollars.

The busiest day of the year for the Mayor of the South Side came every July 1, when the Businessmen's Association would bring the Dominion Day sports to the Athletic Grounds. Jimmy would be all over the place, checking arrangements, improving arrangements. It's said that if you couldn't find anything to slake your thirst at the soft drink stands, you just had to see Jimmy—he would see that you got it. The police were aware of this service but didn't interfere; Jimmy was such a good man to have on your side. At the end of the day, when the last race (human and equine) had been run, Jimmy would hurry up to Whyte Avenue to make arrangements for the big street dance that followed the Dominion Day sports.

Around 1940, Jimmy departed Whyte Avenue for the life of a hotel owner in the country, but he left his former domain with one more legacy. It involved the Sport of Kings. Early on, the Businessmen's Association had decided that racing horses would add zest to the Dominion Day events and went to the provincial government about allowing pari-mutuel betting. Good idea, they were told, but you'll need a charter; just get a lawyer to draw it up. That seemed simple enough, but the plan hit an immediate snag. None of the lawyers they approached could possibly draw up such an impressive document for less than 250 dollars—an amount of which the treasury was approximately 249 dollars short.

The Mayor of the South Side rode to the rescue. From his stock of distiller's art, Jimmy chose a bottle with a distinguished label and called on the lawyer most likely to be persuaded by it. The victim consented to do the charter for fifty dollars, and though there's reasonable doubt that he ever got it, pari-mutuel windows opened on the Athletic Grounds, accepting bets of a lone dollar, not the two demanded across the river at the Exhibition track. It was a comfortable, human-scale touch, of the kind that attracts today's people of the metropolis to Old Strathcona.

The Second World War put a freeze on racing, but the Businessmen's Association retained Jimmy's charter. When the war ended, the charter emerged as Jimmy's sleeping legacy. The Edmonton Exhibition Board was keen to extend the racing season past the fifteen days they were allowed by their own charter. So they rented Jimmy's charter. For forty years thereafter, his legacy paid off in fun and games for Old Strathcona.

SCOUT
Number One

APRIL 24, 1935.

That was the day Lord Baden-Powell came to town. Almost nobody came to Edmonton back then. It's hard to believe now, when getting to London is a mere eight hours by *plane*.

In 1935 Calgary was eight hours by *train*, and Calgary was days from anywhere. So it was an event, a happening, when Lord Baden-Powell, godfather of the Boy Scouts, came on a world tour of the movement he had founded.

We learned about Baden-Powell in school, how he became a hero of the war in South Africa: surrounded by a much larger force of Boers, he had held the town of Mafeking [Mafikeng] for 217 days.

The evening of Baden-Powell's arrival in Edmonton, our Scout troop (and troops and Cub packs from northern Alberta) was to gather in a great rally to hail the chief. Rather than wait for evening to see the hero, I went for a sneak preview when his train pulled into the CPR station, on the site of Railtown today.

The motto of the Scouts is "Be Prepared." I went prepared to see a forbidding, slow-moving man with a face of granite, well on his way to turning into a statue.

I was not prepared for the leprechaun who hopped off the train and went hopping about the platform, radiating delight towards all he met. The hero of Mafeking was no taller than I was. And I was twelve.

In the evening, Scouts and Wolf Cubs swarmed the Exhibition Grounds and the Arena, that crude ancestor of Rexall Place. Designed for cattle shows, the Arena (or Gardens) was home to hockey teams, women's basketball teams, and really big events.

For twenty-five minutes, a band thumped "Colonel Bogey" as troops and packs shuffled out of the north end, past a reviewing stand where our beaming chief took the Scout salute around the boards, and out the north door again, pounding up dust from wood shavings on the dirt floor. We were a ragtag group, in whatever percentage of the uniform parents could afford, parents who were holding off the Depression much as Baden-Powell had held off the foe at Mafeking—keeping the troops busy and healthy and believing in better times ahead.

Another very important person was watching the parade.

In 216 countries around the world today, there are twenty-five million Scouts and leaders—millions of Scouts in a long line leading back to the first camp on Baden-Powell's English estate. The first lad ever to sign up would always be known as Scout Number One.

What were the odds on Scout Number One being in the crowd at the Arena? Further, what odds that he would be an English lord, and a relative of Winston Churchill? And much further, that he would drive to the rally from his farm at Fort Saskatchewan?

George Rodney beat the odds. The oldest son of a baron, he put his name at the head of the list in 1908. By 1919 he had inherited the title Lord Rodney and came to Canada seeking a farm…which he found at Fort Saskatchewan.

Against all odds, Scout Number One was in Edmonton with the Chief Scout on April 24, 1935.

THE

WATER
Music

THERE'S A PRINCIPLE OF PHYSICS that the sound of music is enhanced by water. Though demonstrated most often in the shower, the principle holds true in the great outdoors. The plaint of the loon heard in a wheat field at dawn is a mere curiosity. But carried over the waters of Lake Wabamun at first light, the song is achingly poignant of a time when man lived close to nature. Similarly, the waters of Cooking Lake added layers of enchantment to the sound of bands that played at Lakeview Pavilion. Carried across the murky shallows to a distant canoe, a band's notes became as Glenn Miller's.

The North Saskatchewan River, where it winds through Edmonton, had that power too. In summer evenings, as the nineteenth century rolled into the twentieth, steamboat captains from Prince Albert and the Battlefords liked to have Charlotte Cameron sing on their decks while their boats docked at Fraser's lumber mill along the banks at Riverdale. When D.R. Fraser's great circular saws ceased their daily grind, the scene was so quiet that the voice of the chubby blonde teenager could fill the valley. The voice was not loud but rather had a natural, clear shine which reached the bluffs above. There, people would linger to hear "the old songs."

The Camerons lived in a big house at the top of the street which still bears the Cameron name, a sort of bobsled run dropping steeply to the river. The best river views were claimed by those who came to Edmonton early, and John Cameron arrived in 1881, with a wagonload of merchandise he'd driven all the way from Winnipeg.

This lively photograph shows Walter's ferry leaving the Edmonton shore, bound for Walterdale. The shore-to-shore cable is just out of sight on the right. The two visible cables, attached to the boat fore and aft, adjust the angle of the boat to the current. When the railroad men wanted to stop in midstream, they brought the ferry broadside to the current. With the power of the river distributed

evenly along its side, the ferry hung motionless. When time came to return it, they angled the Walterdale end a few degrees downstream, as seen in the picture. The imbalance created a "parallelogram of forces," another principle of physics, which set the craft moving.

He prospered as a merchant and in other ventures, and gave generously to the community. He was in the group which put up their own money to start a public school system when the Hudson's Bay Company blocked tax-supported schools. He was a member of the first town council and president of the Board of Trade. So, when friends told John: "Really, Charlotte ought to have lessons," there was money for lessons—in New York, in Paris, and in music capitals of Europe.

Charlotte made her career in Europe and assumed a professional name in memory of the hometown where she made her public debut on the river-boats. Audiences came to applaud Madame Edmonti.

Towards midnight on Saturdays in summer, the music scene moved upstream to Walterdale, where the railroad men made a concert platform of John Walter's ferry. (*Railroad men* were the lads who put down tracks; *railroaders* made the trains run.) On Saturdays, the railroad men sought relaxation from muscling one-ton rails and poured into Edmonton. A popular form of relaxation was jumping fully-dressed into the horse trough at Jasper Avenue and 95 Street…a grand spectator sport for kids of the neighbourhood, including, we must suppose, Charlotte Cameron. When Walter's ferry made its last crossing of the night, the railroad men would borrow it, and from midstream bombard the cliffs of Edmonton and Strathcona with rousing ditties and sentimental ballads.

Emotions ran unchecked in songs of the time, with love, requited and otherwise, at the fore. The most popular ballads provided notes that could be dragged out and bawled at top volume with immense satisfaction to the singers. "You're the flah-WER UHHHHHH-VVVV my heart, Sweeeeet Aaaa-duh-liiine, MYYYYYYYYY AAAAAAAA-DOH-LIIIIIIIINE!!!!!" Think of the curious coyotes on the dark hillside howling in fellowship.

The cable ferry is perhaps the "greenest" of all modes of transport, propelled entirely by the forces of the stream it is crossing. A junior high science class could build a working model of Walter's ferry.

For all its thirty-one years on the river, Johnny McFadden was skipper of Walter's ferry. From 1882 till the High Level Bridge opened in 1913, and even nearing the end, the ferry was moving men and machines for the contractor.

Before the bridges were built, Johnny was always willing to challenge the river in aid of young people keen to get to a party on the other side, and he never lost a passenger. Even when ice or flotsam was moving, he took many a group across and home again. He was one of the most durable pioneers, a farmer for six decades. In the ferry years he worked two farms, now known as Windsor Park and Belgravia. The McFadden home on Edinboro Road stood till 1982. In 1944 Johnny was still farming near Ellerslie.

When winter came down from the north, the ferry went into hibernation and traffic crossed the river on ice—for free. But in the awkward seasons, freeze-up and breakup, the ferry cable became a lifeline for Edmonton merchants. Mail went through on a wire strung from the ferry cable. Robertson, the post office driver, reeled it in like laundry from a clothesline, always with an audience.

The opening of the Low Level Bridge in 1900 put an end to this winter attraction. The bridge, first anywhere on the North Saskatchewan River, also put an end to the Lower Ferry and the stewardship of the ferryman, Mr. Durdell (rhymes with Hurdle). Thomas Durdell's age, caution, small stature, and flowing white beard were in vivid contrast to the dashing Johnny McFadden. And Mr. Durdell may have had the clearest conscience in the community—he was almost impossible to rouse when he went to his rest after the last scheduled crossing. Two attempts to get around this difficulty are the stuff of legend. August Johnson was the star of one. He was a railroad man, a contractor. On the night he made history, he arrived at the south bank to find Mr. Durdell irrevocably asleep. Mrs. Johnson, his Irish bride, was on the other side. There's a saying about desperate times. If he couldn't use the ferry, he'd use the cable. He decided to swing hand over hand to the north bank, which didn't seem so far. Away he went. The north bank, however, didn't seem to be getting any closer. It's said that carbohydrates produce energy. With a dark hissing river lapping at your ankles, fear can have the same effect. August Johnson lived to tell the tale, and old-timers were telling it sixty years later.

Then there was the night in 1892 when a bunch of the boys from Edmonton arranged to meet a bunch of the boys from Clover Bar at the

The Low Level Bridge, c. 1910. John Walter's steamboat, *The City of Edmonton*, lies docked at the present-day landing of the *Edmonton Queen*.

Tony Cashman

Strathcona Hotel on Whyte Avenue. They partied well and long, and when they finally headed for home, they arrived at the ferry landing to find Mr. Durdell in a sleep as deep as Snow White's. The boys discussed their problem and realized they really didn't have one. Anybody could run a ferry. Nothing to it. They'd watched a hundred times.

Borrowing a land-locked ferry is hardly piracy on the high seas, but in the spirit of "Yo ho ho and a bottle of rum," they heave-hoed their transportation into the current—and quickly discovered this was not a good idea. Their swashbuckling maneuvering created a parallelogram of forces so powerful that it snapped the connection to the cable and sent the ferry spinning like a leaf among shouts of dismay, recrimination, and profanity.

The runaway scow spun around Riverdale bend, and the bend after that, and after that...till at blessed last it caught on a sandbar...Hurray! Hurray!...on the Edmonton side. We'll leave the boys there, wading to the friendly shore. They're saved. But in the words of their song: They won't get home until morning.

4

THE
OLDEST
Graduate

FOR TWENTY-FIVE YEARS, and another fifteen after he passed to the great convocation in the sky, Thomas Thatcher Grimmett held the record. He was the oldest person to graduate from the University of Alberta. In 1920, at sixty-three, he earned a degree of Bachelor of Laws, with a license to add the letters LL. B. to his name.

Most graduates faded from the scene, but not the oldest. The frail man with the flowing white hair remained a familiar figure on campus and a voice at any meeting of any academic society. It was easy for him to maintain a presence. The campus was only steps from his house in Garneau, the one he bought so his three children could go to university.

Thomas brought the young Grimmetts from Yorkton, Saskatchewan where he'd enjoyed success in business and prestige as a country magistrate. A magistrate had to be a man of substance. When the time came, Thomas had the substance to retire and buy a fine brick house just behind Rutherford House, which was still occupied by A. C. Rutherford, first premier of Alberta and godfather of the university.

With three young Grimmetts enrolled on campus, Thomas decided to join them, laughing off suggestions that he was too old or that going to university at the close of a business career was putting the cart before the horse. He had as much right to higher education as his children—and he was prepared to defend this right. He might have rewritten a famous line by Voltaire to read: "You may not agree with what I have to say, but I will defend to the death *my* right to say it."

Thomas gave notice of this conviction in his freshman year, going against unanimous opposition of his fellow students. An absent-minded professor had forgotten to give an examination on a difficult topic. Thomas's young classmates saw this as good fortune of the highest order, but Thomas would have none of it. He had studied the stuff. He was paying for the course. He had a right to an examination. Despite the protests, he rose and said so. The professor was glad to oblige.

Thomas was not seeking a law degree to join the legal profession, but rather to train in the discipline of organizing and presenting ideas, of which he had many. He would be prepared when he asked the chairman of some society to which he did not belong for permission to speak. The initials LL. B. after his name would be leverage. In the twenty-first century, few can remember the early days of radio in Alberta when Premier Aberhart would broadcast from the Prophetic Bible Institute. He was always introduced as William Aberhart, B. A.

Time has rolled on, rolling right over the campus of Thomas Grimmett. His village of two thousand students has become a city of thirty-six thousand—a quarter of them post-graduates. The campus is now a major transportation hub. In Thomas's day, it was at the end of the most insignificant bus route in Edmonton—a three-block shuttle from the streetcar lines on 109 Street. Beyond the campus lay the forest primeval of Windsor Park.

Today, the old university buildings are boxed in by massive structures constructed in a "Department-of-Public-Works Gothic" style. If these additions could be washed away for just one hour, Thomas's campus would emerge: the Arts Building with Convocation Hall at its core, the Medical Building, the residence halls (Pembina, Athabasca, and Assiniboia), St. Stephen's College, St. Joseph's College, the powerhouse, and the four houses for the president and the deans off in their semi-circle on Saskatchewan Drive.

The campus was remote from the bustle of the city and was shielded further by Garneau, an oasis of trees and gardens in a rather bare landscape. Here lived the professors, doctors, lawyers, judges, and other professionals—neighbours of Thomas Grimmett—with whom he liked to discuss his ideas.

Thomas attended different churches to see if the ministers had worthwhile ideas. One Sunday at a Wesleyan service, he was so impressed by a sermon from Reverend Mr. Ewing that he rose and moved a vote of thanks to the preacher. Thomas also checked the newspapers regularly for notice of any meeting that might be of interest and often asked permission to rise and contribute. He was especially fond of deliberations of the Law Society. Although the chairman might think his contributions a bit long, they were usually worth hearing and often memorable.

Perhaps his best-remembered comment came at one of Mrs. Newton's "peace" meetings. Mrs. Newton was a self-appointed power in all of Thomas Grimmett's years on campus. In 1927, she played CKUA onto the air with Chopin's "Revolutionary Étude" and assumed more responsibilities from 1941 to 1950 when her husband, Dr. Robert Newton, was president of the university. She was for some things and against others, notably smoking. She often had lunch in the campus cafeteria; on those occasions, students weren't allowed to smoke until she had left.

In 1939, with war clouds hovering, Mrs. Newton came out for peace. One of her meetings ended with a resolution urging the Dominion government to stop shipping scrap iron to Japan, a potential enemy. The meeting prepared to adjourn with the comfort of having done some small service for peace. Thomas Grimmett, however, rose to speak: "Ladies and gentlemen, that's a lot of applesauce. You won't stop war by stopping scrap iron going to Japan. You change *human nature* and then maybe you'll have peace."

Some fifteen years after Thomas departed the scene, another student surpassed his achievement of a degree at sixty-three. But the title was not claimed. She didn't care to be known as the oldest graduate.

5

THE

PRINTER'S
Tale

EDMONTON'S OLD-TIMERS HAD STORIES TO TELL. No one had more than Bill Gimblett. Bill was here at the right time, 1907, and in the right place—the composing room of the *Edmonton Bulletin*, where he committed to type history as it happened. It was my good fortune to get to know Bill Gimblett in the 1950s, when he had retired but was allowed to work two days a week and retain his full pension.

Bill had come to the aid of Edmonton's first publisher, Clarence Richards of the Institute of Applied Art, working at an ancient letter press, converting to letters one at a time the words of Jim MacGregor, Grant MacEwan, J.W. Whillans, and myself.

Bill was always in less of a hurry than the publisher to get the books done and out into the marketplace. Progress was slow and could cease altogether if Bill disagreed with the author's version of history. And if he laughed at a story, he would stop to tell some of his own. From these interludes came The Printer's Tale.

The term journeyman, as applied to tradesmen, was never applied to any tradesmen so aptly as it was to printers. From the time the railroads reached Edmonton, it became a port of call for wandering gentlemen of the typesetting trade. A printer riding into Edmonton on the rods never came as a stranger. He knew that somewhere in the composing room of the *Bulletin*, the *Journal*, or the *Daily Capital* there would be printers he had met along the way. He would show his journeyman's card to the boss, and if there was no work he would pass his hat around the shop, take the proceeds to the bar of the Queen's Hotel, and reflect upon his immediate future.

Wandering printers had much of the world's wisdom to draw upon at such a time. Most of the articles, chapters, and editorials they set began or ended with a quotation from Shakespeare or Tennyson or Plutarch or from the greatest book of all. Printers had quotations for every occasion and seemed profound fellows indeed as they rumbled off snippets from the collected wisdom of the world.

"Whiskey Bottle" Jones had a favourite, though he used only the first half. Jones travelled through life with the initials W.B. No one seemed to know what W.B. stood for, so "Whiskey Bottle" came naturally. He kept a small one under the composing rack. When he came to the end of some arduous typesetting for the *Edmonton Bulletin*, he would reach for it, proclaiming, "Man does not live by bread alone." Few of the wandering printers lived by bread alone. They were a thirsty lot, and their thirst was not questioned by management as long as the paper got out on time.

There was only one *Bulletin* manager who took a stern view of thirst on the job. He was brought from Ontario in 1907, where there'd been a little trouble, something about stuffing ballot boxes. But since it was in aid of the Liberal Party, it was not considered such a bad thing. He was at the *Bulletin* for a couple of years till he was elevated to the provincial cabinet of Alberta. Until then, the boys in the composing room got around his "no-thirst-on-the-job" ruling. A couple of times a night, a bucket on a long rope would come down from their second-storey window, and a bartender from the Queen's Hotel would fill the bucket with foaming brew.

On St. Patrick's Day 1907, there was a fire at the *Bulletin*. The presses could be made to run again but that would take weeks, and in the meantime there could be no thought of not publishing—not with the *Journal* attempting to mislead the public with propaganda for the Conservative Party. While the presses were silent, the paper would be typeset as usual at the *Bulletin* building (on the site of today's Shaw Conference Centre) and wheelbarrowed three blocks west to the Edmonton Printing Company (on Rice Howard Way). The route was hazardous, over rough broken sidewalks and unpaved streets made swampy by early spring melting. And halfway there lay another hazard, the swinging doors of the Imperial Hotel.

Because of the Imperial, there are two blank pages in the issue of March 24, 1907. On that fated day, the two boys who had set the type were trundling their work to the printer's. When they paused to rest by the Imperial Hotel, the swinging doors beckoned an irresistible invitation.

The boys agreed they had time to "have one" and still make their deadline. Having had one, they agreed there was time for another. Having had another, they agreed there was time for one more. And having had one more, they decided that if they were quick about it, there was time for still one more. They were quick about it and took up the handles with renewed energy. But the wheelbarrow was barely underway when it showed irreversible symptoms of capsizing. Frantic efforts could not deny the inevitable. They watched helplessly as their missing pages broke into thousands of lead slugs—each representing a letter—and vanished in the mud. They may be there still, under the half-street between the Citadel Theatre and Sun Life Place.

While this slapstick comedy could suggest that chaos ruled the trade, there were signs of stability. Wanderers were still passing through but some were putting down roots, enough to form Local 604 of the International Typographical Union that year. "Whiskey Bottle" Jones was one member. Bill Gimblett was another, along with Guy Deeton, Mel Norman, "Pal" Pallister, and Joe Adair.

Joe Adair was not your ordinary printer. He set many thousands of his own words, crisp and to-the-point in the tone of his native Glasgow. He came to the *Bulletin* in 1906. In 1911 he started a linotype service, which he ran for thirty-five years. In his own shop he was publisher, editor, chief contributor, and cartoonist for "Town Topics."

"Town Topics" was the voice of the "the Ginger Group," concerned citizens who inclined to the view that those who had control of municipal government would steal the steps off city hall if not watched. It was called a "throwaway sheet," which was misleading because it was financed by advertising and placed carefully in bars, barber shops, cigar stores, wherever good fellows met. Public bodies that earned the displeasure of the Ginger Group couldn't ignore Joe carping from the sidelines. He got elected to them: city council three times; the exhibition, library, and public school boards; even the Garneau Home and School Association. And if you needed a magician, Joe Adair could oblige.

The year 1908 brought a union brother from England, lured by words he had helped set in his English print shop, proclaiming the glories—and the ease—of owning a farm in Alberta. He chose a pretty spot near Clyde and discovered quickly, as most English townsmen did, that breaking prairie sod was also backbreaking. Many gave up, but with "British Bulldog" determination he decided he'd stick it out. He'd clear thirty acres a year for three years, build the required log cabin, get title to his homestead, and without delay or ceremony convert it to cash. He spent three summers at hard labour, and each fall he would ride the fifty miles to Edmonton to find a winter's work in his trade. One fall he came riding a steer. If he'd kept on going, he might have made a name at the Calgary Stampede, but he joined the *Journal*, rose to chief in the composing room, and in 1931, 1932, and again in 1933 was elected mayor of Edmonton, in which position his views were not always those of the *Journal*. He was Dan Knott...of Dan Knott School.

In 1919, Local 604 chose not to participate in the biggest labour event of the year. That was the general strike—in sympathy with the general strike that had started in Winnipeg. On May 26 Edmonton union workers walked off the job, except for the printers.

What the strikers thought of Local 604 couldn't be printed in family newspapers like the *Journal* or *Bulletin*. As well, the publishers were using the power of their presses to circulate unflattering opinions of the strikers and the validity of their cause. While indignation mounted on both sides, two striker lads retained their sense of humour. They decided to play a practical joke on the publishers. They can't be identified, to protect reputations earned in later years, but on a dark night they went into the alleys with wire cutters. They shinnied up a pole behind the *Journal* and snipped wires to the pressroom. Then they moved on and performed a similar operation on the *Bulletin*. The joke was that only a licensed electrician was allowed to repair damage to high-tension wires. And the electricians were on strike.

"Whiskey Bottle" Jones would have had words for it.

6

AND THE

WINNER

Is...

SOME STIRRING RACES have quickened the sporting pulse of Edmonton. Man against man. Horse against horse. But 1908 brought a race between a man and a horse, in fact two fast horses. And the horses lost.

Inevitably, a contest so unlikely would beget unlikely aspects. To begin, nobody saw it. It was not held in the presence of a shouting, wagering crowd. And there had to be a prize of course—it was a stand of prize timber in the foot-hills beyond Edson, ideal for chopping into railroad ties. Two contractors spotted it simultaneously. Both were determined to have it. The prize would have to be claimed in Edmonton. It would go to the first man to get there. Another odd aspect: nobody heard about the race till it was over, and even then they didn't hear much. The disgruntled loser was not eager to discuss it, and the winner was a quiet man. All his long life, Swan Swanson was a renowned quiet man.

Quiet though he was, Swan was a young man in a hurry. He grew up amid pine and birch forests in Sweden, working on the family farm in summer and in the family timber operation in winter. At age ten, he could handle the other end of a saw and earn ten cents a day. At fifteen, he was ready for the New World, which meant Minnesota of course, a land of 10,000 lakes and even more Swansons, Olsons, and Johnsons. He arrived there in 1900, to work on trees in winter and construction jobs in summer. Summer work included railroad building and, at twenty-one, he was in Canada working on a line near Moose Jaw. Gossip was all about the two transcontinental railways that were going to be run from Edmonton through the mountains to the sea. That prospect brought him to Edmonton in 1907.

The song "I've Been Working on the Railroad" was almost an anthem for men of Sweden in the New World. Work camps on the mountain lines had a strong Swedish presence and that provided an opening for Carl Berg. On Edmonton's one-hundredth anniversary, Carl was named an Edmontonian of the Century for his contributions to the cause of organized labour. Railroad contactors hired enforcers to keep agitators like Carl out of the camps, but he had a scheme to outwit "the bulls." He walked the rails, introducing himself as the *Reverend* Carl Berg, hoping to conduct a Lutheran service for the Swedes in their own language. The enforcers would hear some rousing Swedish hymns then they'd hear a rousing sermon from Carl, unaware that he was paralleling the Gospel message that the labourer is worthy of his hire.

The action was just beginning when Swan reached Edmonton, but he and his friend Adolf Burklund got an immediate piece of it, a very small piece but a huge learning experience—a subcontract making ties for the railroads. They rounded up a six-man crew in the Swedish boarding houses and hit the trail west, with all their gear on a wagon pulled by a strange team of horses. In assembling this team, they had to substitute ingenuity for capital. They bought a good horse and teamed it with a bucking cayuse which came cheap at the city market. The cayuse fitted in surprisingly well—until it came to hills. Then it would balk and resist all persuasion and have to be practically carried up. Proving themselves more stubborn than the cayuse, Swan's crew eventually reached the area where the future town of Edson would appear, in time for winter.

Logging was a winter occupation. It was easier to move timber on sleighs than on wagons, and farmers and construction workers were at liberty to swing axes. The tie-maker was king of the forest and highest-paid man among the rugged fellows who built the railroads of the west. Trains may have run on rails, but rails ran on ties.

The tie-maker was an artist. He'd choose a tree about a foot thick and bring it down with half a dozen well-aimed blows. He'd lop away the branches, climb aboard the trunk, and walk the length of it, hewing it smooth on one side. Finally, he'd reverse direction and chop away the other side to make the trunk seven inches thick. Then he'd cut it into eight-foot lengths. A good tie-maker could produce fifty a day at seven cents a piece—$3.50 for a day's work. Swan and his crew delivered 2700 ties to the grade, and he and Adolf Burklund split a profit of 500 dollars.

As the next season approached, they landed a much bigger contract, took in a third partner, Ole Hansen, and set out for Edson with a party of twenty-five Swedes and one Englishman, reputed to be a cook. Trailing the wagons came a couple of steers. The bosses couldn't afford dressed beef, so the meat supply had to walk too.

At their destination, Swan spotted the perfect stand of timber, only two miles from the grade. He prepared to go back to Edmonton to register his claim at the Dominion Lands and Crown Timber Office.

Though Alberta was now a province, Ottawa still controlled our natural resources "in the national interest." Swan exulted in his discovery, but as fortune would have it, a bigger operator with a bigger contract discovered it too. The man who got to Edmonton first would claim the prize.

Swan couldn't travel by train; the rails had reached only to Stony Plain. Nelson, the big operator, had a light buggy with two fast horses, but Swan had two secret weapons—his feet. The stage was set for a contest that would make his career.

When Nelson announced that he would start the next morning, Swan played "the quiet man," but as night closed in on the forest, he slipped away down the trail to Edmonton. At daybreak, when his rival was ready to move, Swan was more than twenty miles in the lead.

He walked into the first day at a swift but unhurried pace. He knew he had certain advantages. On the rough trail, with bogs to skirt and streams to cross, including the steep slash of the Pembina River, fast horses could make no better time than equines of the working class. They couldn't take short-cuts that Swan could, and couldn't go twenty-one hours a day as he could, with only three hours for sleep.

He walked into the second night and into the second day and into the third night with no sighting of his pursuers. At the end of the third night, while the city slept, he was walking the streets of Edmonton, down Jasper

Avenue, past the end of the streetcar tracks at 116 Street, one more mile to go. The Crown Timber Office was at 105 Street. Swan was there seven hours ahead of Nelson's horses.

The race went more smoothly than winter among the trees. Food was a problem. The Englishman couldn't cook; then half the meat supply took off into the bush, and Swan had to spend two days catching it. There was little snow that season, which complicated getting ties to the grade. The boys might start in snow piling ties onto a sleigh and piling a wagon on top of all, and then they'd come to a half-mile of open ground. That meant taking down the wagon, moving the ties from the sleigh to the wagon, then hoisting the sleigh to the top. This worked till they came to another stretch of snow, and the gruelling process had to be reversed. Yet they persevered. They delivered 30,000 ties and Swan's share of the profits was two thousand dollars.

Before the next season, Swan was busy—in his quiet way. He met and married a Swedish lovely named Lydia Anderson. Lydia became his business partner too, in a stopping house at Wildwood. The first trains had no dining cars and ran to no recognizable schedule. At any hour, Lydia could expect a carload of passengers to come trooping in, calling for flapjacks, bacon, and eggs.

Meanwhile, Swan had ties to deliver—twenty million eventually, enough to carry the rails from Edmonton to Winnipeg, complete with sidings. Or, laid end to end, run one-and-a-quarter times around the world. And that was only part of the business of the Swanson Lumber Company, which was on the scene till conglomeration in 1969. The achievement of a quiet man who had no need to talk the talk. He just walked the walk.

7

THE
OFFICIAL
Gazette

"THE MAN WHO WROTE THAT EDITORIAL is a candidate for the title of champion liar of the Northwest!" So said Mayor Billy McNamara at a council meeting in March 1914, waving a copy of the *Bulletin*, one of Edmonton's three daily papers. The *Bulletin* was against the Conservatives. The *Journal* was against the Liberals. The *Capital*, the labour paper, was against the capitalists. All seemed to be against city council, and not just the dailies but throwaway sheets like "Town Topics" and "The Ram's Horn."

These were turbulent times. The first boom opened with the inauguration of the province in 1905 and closed with the war in 1914. There were few shrinking violets among the young boosters who left the comfort of established places to build a city and personal fortunes on a patch of prairie. In the tumult, the boosters subdivided enough farms to give Edmonton the area of Chicago—with population soon to follow. Population did follow, but not soon. When the boom ended, it was somewhere between 54,000 conceded by the federal census and 72,516 claimed by the boosters.

During this time, the city councillors were often against each other. On the night Mayor Billy McNamara announced his choice for champion liar, one councillor was heard to tell another: "I'll kill you. I'll kill you sure as you're a foot tall if you say that again!" Weeks later, Mayor McNamara and Alderman Joe Clarke livened the agenda with fisticuffs over what each was alleged to have said about the other during an investigation of the police.

While the dailies and "Town Topics" were against city hall in general, the editor of "The Ram's Horn" was against one alderman in particular.

A.G. Ridgway chose a powerful symbol for his masthead: the non-ferrous trumpet of Biblical times, which could be sounded as a call to prayer or a warning that skulduggery was afoot. Mr. Ridgway subjected his targets to poetry and prose that would be considered cruel and unusual punishment in a prison. His obsession was Alderman Gus May, of whom he asked his readers: "Is this jink of humanity the best product our city can send to manage its affairs? No wonder we get such results. We continue to be represented by toys and guttersnipes who would never otherwise be heard of."

Despite Mr. Ridgway's prediction, Gus and his brother-in-law Percy Byron would leave a name for themselves in Edmonton. Percy was the son of a famed New York photographer. He came to Edmonton in 1906 and set up a photo and engraving shop. Gus joined him the next year. Business flourished. They had sixteen employees, and Gus entered politics. Of course, the boom didn't last. By the early 1920s, Gus and Percy were back on Broadway, where Percy became as famous as his father—photographer to the celebrities and the French steamship line. He was invited to record maiden voyages of such beauties as the *Normandie* and *Ile de France*. Departing Edmonton, Byron and May left behind some fifteen hundred images of the city in its first rush of turbulent youth. For decades, this legacy sat in a backroom of McDermid Studios, gathering dust except when someone pawed through it to find a print they liked and purchased it for fifty cents or a dollar. On this carefree basis, the collection survived till it became historic and was lodged in the Glenbow Archives. The brand Byron & May on a photo is a certificate of excellence, a vote of appreciation for Percy Byron and that jink of humanity, Gus May.

Having nominated the *Bulletin's* editorial writer for champion liar of the Northwest, Billy McNamara did not drop the matter but went on to what could be done about it. The people couldn't hope to learn what was going on at city hall from distorted reports in the newspapers. The people should have an *Official Gazette* in which they could read complete, fair, uncoloured, unbiased reports. New York had an official gazette. So did Denver—he produced a copy. Edmonton should have one.

Enthusiasm ran high and was tempered only when someone brought up the question of how much it would cost. Billy was ready with the answer.

Production would take $18,000, but the true cost would be only $7,000, because the city would save the $11,000 a year that it had been paying to lying newspapers to advertise bylaws, local improvement schedules, and legal notices. Now these would be advertised in the *Official Gazette*. The best part was citizens would obtain those complete, fair, uncoloured, unbiased reports for nothing. There was a junior clerk in the commissioners' office who could write. The *Gazette* would be added to his duties.

His bosses would have guffawed if they'd been told that this junior clerk was destined to be a distinguished Canadian, that he would become a lawyer, law partner of R.B. Bennett, general counsel for United Grain Growers, national spokesman for the arts, first chairman of the Canadian Broadcasting Corporation in 1936, confidante and speechwriter for Mackenzie King, and an inspiring spokesman for Canadian identity. Back in 1914, however, Leonard W. Brockington was an undistinguished Welshman. Bob English, the commissioners' secretary who hired him, recalled years later that young Brockington's amazing powers of forceful expression rose above his unkempt appearance.

The maiden issue of the *Gazette* hit the streets on March 19, 1914 with a pledge "to set before the citizens an official statement of the activities of the various civic departments, and an accurate account of the deliberations of their council and commissioners." It was read avidly—at the dailies. The *Capital* called it "a vile specimen of a newspaper...future generations will see it in the chamber of horrors of some school of journalism."

The dailies jumped with glee on the *Gazette's* report of a council meeting on March 17. There was no meeting that day. Accurate? Hah! Complete? Complete fabrication.

It was a setback for the editor, but he soldiered on and used photography to brighten the pages—and the dailies couldn't possibly accuse the camera of lying. No, the camera couldn't lie, but it could aid and abet the private interests of certain aldermen. Certain aldermen had real estate to sell in scenic Capital Hill. On May 7, the *Gazette* featured a nice spring photo of a baseball game at Diamond Park. The *Bulletin* saw through it: no less than three aldermen were using the *Gazette* for private gain. One had an interest in the ball park, another in the team, and the photo was engraved in the studio of a third, Gus May.

Leonard Brockington's literary flair put the city in potential legal tangles. For example, there were frequent plebiscites in which property owners voted yes or no to propositions put forward by the council. The questions had to be advertised in the *Gazette*. Leonard found the words of council resolutions to be dull and tedious, so he rewrote them in the pungent English of which he was master. The lacklustre words of the councillors, however, appeared on the ballots. There is reasonable doubt that the bylaws were ever advertised as required.

The circus became too much for some prominent citizens who went to court seeking an injunction to stop the publication of the *Gazette*. Three ex-mayors were in the group—John A. McDougall, Robert Lee, and Billy Griesbach. They argued that publishing a newspaper was beyond the powers of a municipal corporation; that the *Gazette* was created to promote the interests of a certain clique of aldermen; that it was not in the bona fide interest of the city; and that it was a waste of money.

The complaint was important enough to be heard by Chief Justice Harvey. The only point over which he had jurisdiction, however, was whether publishing a newspaper was beyond the powers of a municipal corporation. He ruled that it was not. The *Gazette* gave the decision considerably more play than the *Bulletin*, the *Journal*, or the *Capital* and continued week after week, complete, fair, uncoloured, unbiased. Well, complete anyway. The *Gazette's* bitterest detractors would not deny it was complete. It reported everything. Committee meetings. Claims against the city for $2.15 to repair a coat damaged by a nail in a streetcar. Every cheque disbursed: from W. Rae $1.25 to Sinking Fund $99,312.14. The *Gazette* had absolutely everything— so much so that when the row about its existence calmed down, people lost interest. By July, the *Bulletin* was pleased to announce that more copies were being delivered to the incinerator than to the citizens. With the issue of July 30, 1914, the *Official Gazette* was officially dead.

8

THE
Scariest Place
IN
TOWN

ED KELLY ENJOYED TELLING ABOUT IT. Ed was born in Edmonton in 1887, so he was an authority on being a kid here in the last days of the nineteenth century. There weren't many people, but the town was extraordinarily well off for Kellys.

The first Kellys were Ed's father John and his Uncle Luke, who arrived in Edmonton in 1880, leaving six younger siblings and their parents on the family farm in Glengarry County, Ontario. John was an engineer; one of the founders of the first electric light service. Luke opened a hotel in the region of 97 Street and Jasper Avenue, the first to be called "The Alberta."

When their father died in 1883, the older brothers decided the whole family should be in Edmonton. They planned to give them a grand entrance to the west. The CPR was building a railway across the prairies, but trains were running only to Swift Current. The Kellys would rendezvous in Winnipeg, and all would travel to Edmonton on the steamboats, flat-bottomed stern-wheelers in the Mississippi River style. The steamboat was the genteel way to travel.

They would sail down the Red River and up Lake Winnipeg to the Grand Rapids, where waters of the Saskatchewan River fall one hundred feet into the lake down a cataract three miles long. Above the rapids, they would board the grandest steamboat of them all, the *Northwest*, a floating palace costing $27,000 to build, with two bridal suites and a $5,000 grand piano. The *Northwest* was two hundred feet long. Steel stacks towered sixty feet above the landscape through which it passed. There was plenty of deck space for the younger children to run and play. The older boys could shoot at wild game when the boat ran close to the bank. There would be action to watch when the boat tied up to take on wood or unload freight. It would be a nice rest for their mother. The Kellys would begin their new life in the west on a ten-day cruise.

It was a journey from heaven. Sadly, the family's westward trek turned into a journey from the other place. Out of the clear blue prairie sky, the boat's owners announced an increase in prices. With higher costs of labour and food, meals would have to be fifty cents apiece. At those rates, the Kellys would be mighty hungry before the boat tied up under the bluffs of Edmonton. Luke had to get back to run the hotel, so it was decided that he would go up by the boat and John would bring the others by train and wagon.

Train fares went up too. There was money for only four of the children, so Bill and Charlie rode as stowaways in a boxcar with the family belongings. At Swift Current, all piled onto a wagon. Mother's nice rest became ten nights of camping in the open. On Dominion Day 1883, they reached journey's end, adding seven Kellys to the population of Edmonton.

A couple of years later, John made a Kelly of Georgina Voisey, a niece of Father Lacombe. There was some turbulence about the match. For some reason, the grand old missionary didn't think as highly of John as Georgina did. In such cases, however, love usually prevails, and in 1887 the Edmonton settlement was blessed with another Kelly, named Ed, with six more to follow.

Ed grew up to be a consultant to the petroleum industry on geological deposits, and on what it was like to be a child here as the nineteenth century made way for the twentieth. There wasn't much action in town, but the Kellys lived katercorner from whatever there was: the combined fire hall, police station, and town office (on 98 Street, the present site of Canada Place). If the fire bell clanged in the middle of the night, from his bedroom window, Ed would watch the volunteer brigade scramble.

Ed's school days began in the one-room school which was big enough for the entire system...and which, after sixty years as a family home in

Rossdale, was restored to its place of pride overlooking the river valley. Today, yellow buses pull up there so that kids five generations later can relive Ed's experience.

One of Ed's most memorable days came in winter. There was fresh snow on the ground, of a consistency ideal for snowballs. Ed was outside the school. A kid inside raised one of the six windows and hurled an insult. Ed had a snowball ready to launch. He threw it at the open window. As it left his hand—beyond recall—his tormentor banged the window shut. Helpless, Ed watched the glass shatter. Seconds later, the teacher came storming out the door.

Ed had to pay for the window. It wasn't such a problem for him because he had a job—in spring, summer, and fall anyway. He herded cows. Many families had a cow. The Alberta Hotel had two to provide fresh milk and cream for the dining room. Ed would get up early, collect Uncle Luke's milk supply and the rest of the herd and lead them to a pasture around the site of today's Grant MacEwan College (main campus). The only problem was his horse. Nellie was so tall that if Ed got off for any reason, he couldn't get back up again. So, he'd lead Nellie into the handiest patch of woods, tie her to a tree, and when time came to remount, he'd climb the tree and drop down on her broad back.

The kid's town Ed Kelly described seemed a realm of sunshine and friendly woods, but there was a scary place that he told about. The Kellys lived east of 101 Street, as most people did, yet there were a few houses west of that street. Edmonton was beginning to grow a west end. If Ed went to visit a friend out there and was coming home after dark, he had to go past the spookiest place in town. Darkness was absolute on nineteenth-century nights, no reassuring streetlights to temper the menacing gloom. Whenever Ed came within a block of the scariest place, he felt fear agitate the roots of his hair and propel his feet into an anxious trot. Speed mounted in direct proportion to fright. Feet flew in a deadly race against pursuing terrors until he could pull up gasping, safely past the scariest place in town: the cemetery at First Street and Jasper Avenue.

The Scariest Place in Town, fifty years later. In 1943 a streetcar bound for North Edmonton grinds past 101 Street, now the busiest intersection in town. On the left of the picture the Bank of Montreal stands on the site of the scary cemetery. Behind Car 61 looms the Selkirk Hotel, now replicated in

Fort Edmonton Park, and along Jasper Avenue the Empress Theatre, Heintzmann's music house, Johnstone Walker's department store, and the American Dairy Lunch.

Lady Aberdeen

PLAYS

EDMONTON

ON OCTOBER 13, 1894, on her first visit to Edmonton, Lady Aberdeen, wife of the governor general, liked what she saw: "Pretty scenery with plenty of timber, very different from the dreary prairies."

She also expressed what she saw in a water colour titled *Edmonton from South Edmonton*. The fall colours are correct, not Ontario-red. Her easel must have been set on Saskatchewan Drive, near today's Faculty Club. The Hudson's Bay Company trading fort appears at the right, on a shoulder of the high bluff. The few buildings trail away to the north and west. The river in the foreground is confusing—a graceful bend where the stream runs straight. The alteration may be covered by artistic license or perhaps by vice-regal prerogative. This right was invoked by a later governor general, Ray Hnatyshn, on the golf course. Having muffed his drive, he declared a provisional mulligan. "You can't do that," said his playing partners, "the *provisional* mulligan is not in the rules of golf." He announced: "I'm the governor general. I can make any rule I want."

Lady Aberdeen, daughter of a Scottish peer, made her own rules when she came to Ottawa. While the governor general's consort was expected to engage in the social life of the capital, she plunged into the social conditions of the whole country. She was an unapologetic reformer, an advocate for the rights and aspirations of women, children, and the poor, igniting a torch for Emily Murphy, Nellie McClung, and the rest of the Famous Five. When zeal for a cause carried Lady Aberdeen beyond the parameters of political or diplomatic correctness, she enjoyed the support of her husband, John

Campbell Hamilton Gordon, seventh earl of Aberdeen. (His family had been in Canada before; an uncle was lieutenant-governor of New Brunswick at the time of Confederation.) Lady Aberdeen's action-packed idealism created two permanent institutions: the National Council of Women and the Victorian Order of Nurses (VON). The VON formed in Edmonton in 1906 and still brings nursing care to people in their homes.

In August 1898, the Aberdeens came again, on their farewell tour, and town boosters were determined to show them the progress Edmonton had made in four years. The governor general would want to hear about the black bear that Billy Vogel the butcher had shot in Mill Creek Ravine. The governor general's family were avid sportsmen, which, for Scottish aristocrats, meant shooting and fishing. There was a fish story told about his grandfather, the fourth Lord Aberdeen, British prime minister from 1853 to 1855. In 1846, as foreign secretary, he negotiated with the United States a treaty to settle the boundary dispute in the far west of North America. It was alleged by his friends that he agreed to the proposed boundary because "salmon would not take the fly south of the 49th Parallel"—a story which deserves to be true though it possibly may not be.

The boosters made absolutely sure their vice-regal visitors would see the sights of Edmonton, especially because a month earlier a trainload of American journalists had got away without that experience. One hundred sixty-nine writers in five Pullman cars were touring the west, guests of the Canadian Pacific Railway, on the tacit understanding that they would return to Wisconsin and Michigan to convey to their readers the joys of taking up CPR land on Canada's golden prairies—the Last Best West. Because the train could come only as close as Strathcona, and was to arrive in the early morning, Edmonton's town councillors hired rigs to meet them, bring them down Scona Hill, and across the river on the lower ferry. The train arrived mid-morning instead, so when the journalists finally reached Edmonton, they needed breakfast. They piled out of the rigs and into the hotels. With breakfast accomplished, they piled into the bars. And when they came piling out of the bars, they had to hurry to catch their free train. While the train pulled away, they cried: "Three cheers for Alberta!" (even though it was still but a provisional district) and sang "God Save the Queen," leaving disgruntled boosters on the platform. The boosters wouldn't let *that* happen again.

The vice-regal tour began as planned at the North West Mounted Police Barracks (95 Street and Jasper Avenue) and proceeded west toward the biggest man-made object on the skyline, the General Hospital—four storeys of red brick at 100 Avenue and 112 Street. If Lady Aberdeen had painted her picture on the second visit, the hospital would have required recognition. For transportation, the boosters hired a landau with Mr. and Mrs. Nicholas Beck as tour conductors. Mr. Beck was already something of a local legend, the town solicitor who drew up the bylaw making it illegal to ride a bicycle on the sidewalk and became the first citizen convicted of the offense, a misdemeanour that didn't prevent his rise to the Supreme Court of Alberta.

Their Excellencies experienced sights the journalists had rushed off without seeing. There was no pavement to be seen on the streets, not even the main street, but just north of Jasper Avenue on 98 Street stood the hub of civic government, two storeys of red brick with a bell tower, a combination fire hall, police station, and jail, with town offices above. In the town clerk's office, the visitors saw drawings of imminent progress. Specifications for the Low Level Bridge were inspected, for which tenders for construction would be received up to September 13. Edmonton was to shed its dependence on ferries for crossing the river.

On the south side of Jasper Avenue stood the Post Office, which handled the third most business in the Northwest Territories, the governor general was advised. Alex Taylor was the postmaster. He also owned the telephone exchange on the floor above, from which wires carried through a box frame on the roof to a parade of forty-foot poles to the Hudson's Bay Company store at 103 Street.

By the door of the Post Office, Alex had posted the voters list for a coming plebiscite on prohibition. It had a total of 501 names. The editor of the *Bulletin* cautioned that this figure gave a misleading impression of Edmonton's true size. For that you had to add the people who couldn't vote—women, children, latecomers, Aboriginals, and the Gold Rush crowd.

Klondike fever was running high. In the window of C.W. Mathers's photo studio was a sign: Typical Views of Edmonton Mailed to Any Address in the World, 65 Cents. The typical view on display showed a band of young adventurers outfitting for the long trail.

The scenic route then veered towards the river and west along MacDonald Drive and 100 Avenue. Passing 101 Street, there were two things to see. On one side, the Reverend George McDougall's original mission church (now in Fort Edmonton Park). On the other, down in Rossdale by the river, was the town power plant, owned by Alex Taylor. Though the construction couldn't be seen from this distance, the governor general would want to know that a major expansion was in progress. The plant burned coal... Edmonton coal, none better. With only two boilers, when one was out of service for cleaning, the town was reduced to half power; light bulbs would glow dimly. Mr. Taylor was fixing that by installing a third boiler.

The landau rolled up 100 Avenue towards the most *official* sight on the tour, the Dominion Government Building at 106 Street—one storey of stolid red brick, top heavy with a chateau roof. In this miniature fortress (later used as Victoria Armoury), the federal power conducted its principal business in the west: the granting of land titles. To people as far off as eastern Europe, the prospect of secure title to a quarter-section of land was as attractive as Yukon gold to young adventurers. Strange that the Land Titles Office, which placed its stamp on so many thousand family histories, is still there, intact but unnoticed, under shadows of skyscrapers and a wash of pallid green stucco applied by the government of Alberta.

The Land Titles Office was the government's business. The carriage rolled on toward the General Hospital, which was nobody's *business* but an act of charity by the Grey Nuns. To make the town's health centre accessible, the Works Committee had run a sidewalk to it, wooden of course, elevated to raise footwear beyond the reach of winter snows, spring floods, and summer mud.

The hospital was in sight. The tour had gone as planned but the Beck family home was close by and they were worried about the children—not about their safety, but whether they would do what they were told not to do. The four young Becks—Beatrice, Marjorie, Cyril, and Austin—were told that when the distinguished visitors passed by, they must stand on the sidewalk and cheer. They must not rush the carriage shouting: "There's Mummy and Daddy." That would detract from the dignity of the occasion, not to mention Mummy's and Daddy's.

The children were in sight, on the sidewalk waving their flags. Then they forgot. They were rushing the carriage shouting: "There's Mummy and Daddy!"

Confusion reigned. No one knew what to do...except Lord and Lady Aberdeen. They accorded the excited intruders the utmost joviality. It's a safe bet that long after they forgot the wonders of Edmonton, the visitors remembered Beatrice, Marjorie, Cyril, and Austin.

10

Lady Aberdeen—
THE SEQUEL

THERE CAN BE LITTLE DOUBT that upholders of the status quo wished Lady Aberdeen would go away. But she wouldn't. In 1909 she was back in Canada, in Toronto, to chair a meeting of the International Council of Women. This gathering declared that women's suffrage was a right.

In 1931, when Lady Aberdeen was living in retirement in Scotland, writing and illustrating children's books, the memory of her farewell to Edmonton was so alive that a group of local women formed the Lady Aberdeen League. The league provided the Victorian Order of Nurses with office equipment and a car for home visits. The league also helped hospitals during the Great Depression, supplying surgical dressings, rolled bandages, and knitted baby clothes. This was at a time when nuns from the General Hospital had to put unpaid bills behind the statue of St. Joseph and go in and out of stores on Jasper Avenue with a collection basket. In wartime, the league responded to wounded veterans at the Mewburn Pavilion of the University Hospital by supplying hundreds of books and the salary of a librarian. When the league disbanded in 1996, its farewell act was to present a TV/VCR to the Youth Emergency Shelter. Lady Aberdeen would have liked that.

11

MISSION
Improbable

"AND NOW FOR SOMETHING COMPLETELY DIFFERENT" could introduce the story of St. Faith's Anglican Church. What other church was founded by seventeen missionaries? It happened in 1910, when a group of adventurous idealists, newly ordained, answered the call of the Archbishop of Canterbury to serve three years in the Edmonton Mission, much as young British army officers and up-and-coming civil servants were expected to served an apprenticeship in the Empire.

Citizens of Edmonton, a proud capital with a population of 20,000-plus (growing with each arriving train), would contend that their city had outgrown mission status, but the mission field began at the city limits, extending outwards in any direction where a pocket of Anglican settlers, too small to build a church or support a resident minister, would welcome an ordained visitor.

As a base for the mission, the church acquired a half-block in Norwood, a neighbourhood with a rather racy history—south of Alberta Avenue from Lorne to Kennedy Streets, south of 118 Avenue from 92 to 93 Streets.

The first order of business for the gallant seventeen missionaries was a stable for the horses that would carry them to their scattered congregations. They slept in the hayloft and built a headquarters for themselves.

A city neighbourhood was building up quickly in the open spaces around. There were soon enough Anglicans to form the parish of St. Faith's. The parish needed a house of worship, so a wing was detached from the new headquarters, put on rollers and moved sixty feet north. The parishioners then tacked on another fifty feet. On July 18, 1913, the bishop of Calgary came to dedicate the temporary church. After the brave beginning, unforeseeable circumstances intervened to produce a new definition of temporary. The real estate boom collapsed. War broke out. The missionaries went home to join the chaplain service. Battalions of young Edmontonians marched away, one thousand at a time. Investment capital dried up. The temporary church would serve through the First World War, the Great Depression, the Second World War, and well into the oil boom.

The faithful of St. Faith's were certainly adaptable. The missionaries' stable was adapted to provide a Sunday School and club house for the youngest parishioners. In 1916, the need of a parish hall inspired the acquisition of a vacant store facing on the avenue. It was in such dire need of paint that the vestry made a deal with one of the packing plants. The packers would paint the inside and then be free to decorate the outside with a garish multicoloured ham, perhaps the first mural on Alberta Avenue. The wooden building shook when occupied, raising the question: Will the roof or the floor cave in first? But the hall served for thirty-two years, and even after that was incorporated into the tin-works of the Upright Brothers. Through the slow "temporary" years, the most prominent feature of the property was an excavation—60 feet wide and 104 feet long. It was created between 1914 and 1915, when the pioneers decided they could show a start on the permanent church and bring some employment to the neighbourhood. A man could earn forty cents digging a cubic yard of dirt, to a maximum of six dollars a week. Phase one was accomplished in weeks; phase two had to wait four decades.

The interim church was small; 150 people could get in with difficulty, but wind and rain got in with ease. Once, when wind shook the building and sprayed rain through the cracks, Canon Newton announced that the next hymn would be "For Those in Peril on the Sea."

At other times, the wind would fail—for the organ. The bellows man was an essential partner of the organist. He had a habit of falling asleep if the sermon failed to hold his attention. When that happened, the choir would have to sing the offertory hymn a cappella.

These inside stories come courtesy of Canon Fred Clough (Cluff), pastor from 1923 until 1940, when he was called to serve as chaplain in his second world war. The Canon was the right man for the time, a time of economic and psychological depression, one of the most genial, understanding men ever to walk our streets. He was fond of young people, and his parents must have been too. Fred was the thirteenth of thirteen children born to the Clough family in the Pennine Hills of northern England. The only time he ever refused the young people anything was when the Scout master wanted to build them a rifle range in the church basement.

In Canon Clough's time, St. Faith's Anglican Church, the Alberta Avenue Community League, and the Maple Leaf Athletic Club were all of a piece. When the war ended and the oil boom began, the historical buildings were still in use. The old mission headquarters was being transformed into Elizabeth House, a residence for senior ladies very much in the English style. The year 1957 was one of fulfillment. The basement excavated with faith, hope, and charity during the First World War could finally have a permanent church built over top of it. After forty-four years, the temporary church could blend into the century of memories, including the small events which tell a bigger story. The collective memory is also a procession of people, led by the seventeen young clerics whose beliefs brought them from England and, in 1914, took them home again to join the chaplain service. Ten of the founders of St. Faith's would die in France.

RENÉ
Lemarchand

IN 2010, THE RENÉ LEMARCHAND MANSIONS will mark a century of gracious living. There are many remarkable things about the Beaux Arts building on 100 Avenue at 116 Street, but none more remarkable than the man who built it.

René Lemarchand arrived from Paris about 1905. Some men came to Edmonton to make their fortunes, but he brought one, and a most remarkable fortune it was. Lemarchand was a very short man, but impressive—very portly, very courtly. The perfect Parisian, his presence could transform a mud street into a boulevard. He was probably the most polite man to grace the boulevards. He would listen to people with such grave, unwavering politeness that observers thought he must doubt what he was hearing.

In Paris, Lemarchand had been butler to a gentleman of great wealth and exacting taste, so exacting about his morning shave that he insisted on a new razor each day. This was the era of the straight razor, when most men owned three or four in a lifetime and sharpened them for each operation. This gentleman, however, could afford his eccentricity, and Lemarchand the butler dismissed it with a traditional Gallic shrug. Over the years, thousands of razors of impeccable design piled up. The truism that "you can't take it with you" applies to razors as well. When the gentleman passed on, he left them all to his butler. Lemarchand decided he would come to Canada and go into business selling them. He chose Edmonton because his brother, the Oblate missionary Father Lemarchand, was pastor of St. Joachim's Church. René came with his wife and three daughters. The Lemarchands opened a shop on Jasper Avenue,

The René Lemarchand Mansions, 1912.

Glenbow Archives NC 6-209

west of 102 Street, on the south side. They sold elegant razors and fine china and silver imported from their native France, dealing them off to the public with Parisian flair. Every Sunday, René drove a fine team of black horses to church. He was the picture of Parisian elegance, from his patent leather shoes to his top hat.

Along with other men of imagination and spirit, he was soon dealing in real estate. In Henderson's Directory, his occupation was listed as *capitalist*, but even in the hustle of the land boom he never lost his Parisian style. When negotiating a deal, he had to translate the dollars and cents into francs and centimes before he could grasp its significance. His landmark exercise in francs and centimes created the René Lemarchand Mansions.

He'd been here three years when he decided that he must build the most elegant apartment house west of Toronto. He called in Alfred Calderon, the jovial English architect who designed the Edmonton Club and the administration buildings at Jasper Park, and told him what he wanted: a four-storey building with forty-three apartments. He wanted every room to have direct daylight and every suite to have an electric dumbwaiter to the basement—so there would be no tradesmen in the corridors delivering vegetables. He wanted the building to have gas heating. Since natural gas was not yet widely available, the place must have its own gas plant in the basement. The building also had to be the first apartment block in Edmonton with an elevator.

No expense was to be spared. From a distance, observers were to recognize an outpost of Paris overlooking the North Saskatchewan River, an architectural gem of the Beaux Arts school. Calderon translated Lemarchand's ideas into a design that would dominate the west-end skyline. Calderon said it would cost 200,000 dollars.

To comprehend the magnitude of his vision, Lemarchand converted 200,000 dollars to francs in his head and set out for Paris to raise 1,036,800 francs. The one-time butler had a surprising source of finance, the Union Garcons de Café. The Union of Café Waiters controlled a big investment fund. He persuaded them to take the first mortgage on the most elegant apartment house west of Toronto.

The René Lemarchand Mansions opened in August 1910. The least expensive mansions (the three-room suites) rented for fifty-five dollars a month. They were a great success and reason for civic pride, but success did not change René, or make him any less polite.

Lemarchand's friends once took advantage of his politeness to keep him out of danger. In 1916, he announced that he must make a trip to France. His friends tried to talk him out of it; they warned him about enemy submarines. He thanked them for their concern, but said, with a Gallic shrug, that he must go. All right, if he must go, they would tender him a bon voyage banquet. Lemarchand said he would be happy to attend but the function must end no later than ten-thirty for he must catch his train at eleven o'clock. The train would get him to New York with one hour to catch his boat. All right, the boys promised that the occasion would end no later than ten-thirty. The Macdonald Hotel served a fine dinner, then the friends got up and made speeches about what a fine fellow Lemarchand was, what a good citizen, a friend to all, a shining light of his church, how much he had done for his adopted city, how much they would miss him. They talked on and on about the grand fellow. Too polite to interrupt, he sat and listened till he missed his train and his boat. Just as his friends had planned.

13

GLAD
Tidings

IN THE ALBERTA CENTENNIAL CELEBRATIONS of 2005, another centennial was overlooked, one hundred years of gladiolas in Edmonton. Ironically, the man who introduced the gladiolas led off the inaugural celebration of 1905. The Mounted Police were to fire an official twenty-one gun salute on the afternoon of August 1, but Tommy Irvine and two Irish friends literally and figuratively jumped the gun. They decided to herald the great day with an unofficial salute at midnight. They borrowed an historic signal cannon from the Hudson's Bay Company, bought gunpowder, and asked their landlady to sew powder bags on her machine. As the witching hour approached, they assembled their artillery in a vegetable garden. At midnight, they fired an unofficial twenty-one gun salute.

The garden was at the foot of McDougall Hill, where Tommy was renting a greenhouse from Donald Ross. Ross was the founder of Rossdale, Edmonton's first hotelkeeper, first commercial vegetable man, et cetera. Tommy Irvine had a number of irons in the fire—freelance photographer, newspaper writer, and real estate with Del Grierson of Grierson Hill. In the spring of 1905, he decided to rent a greenhouse from Donald Ross and planned to sublet it at a profit.

When Tommy couldn't find a tenant, he thought he'd try running the greenhouse himself. Ross started him with a bag of seeds and bulbs. It was the famous "five dollars bag" offered by Childs and Company of New York, a huge surprise package in which you get more than five dollars' worth of whatever Childs and Company put into it. Irvine and Ross recognized everything in their bag except ten bulbs marked *gladiolus*. Though Ross was a gifted horticulturist and friend of Luther Burbank, the greatest plant breeder of the time, Ross had never heard of gladiolus.

Tommy planted the ten bulbs. Only one bloomed, but that was enough to catch him for life. His gladiolas looked something like an iris; he was not surprised to learn that it was developed from the iris. The name of this lush poetic plant is rooted in marital arts: the long spikes suggest the swords, or gladioli, wielded by Roman warriors in the arena.

There was a flower show that summer, in a tent on a vacant lot at Jasper Avenue and 104 Street. Tommy's entry was the only gladiolus among the potted geraniums and other flowers in pots. It received the attention and disbelief of Frank Oliver. The great editor-statesman glared at the clusters of luminous flowers blooming from bottom to top along willowy spikes. "Irvine, where did this thing come from?"

"Why, I grew it right here, down in Donald Ross's greenhouse."

"Irvine, you're a goddam liar. You couldn't grow that here. I don't believe there is such a thing."

The Wright brothers, Marconi, and other men-ahead-of-their-time were battling scepticism. Like them, Tommy persevered, and he told the Frank Oliver story many times through the next sixty-some years while he pursued his lifelong hobby and quest. He developed a strain for the short Edmonton season, one which blossoms in sixty-five days. He named it *Patricia Culley*, for a little girl who had been intrigued by the fairytale plant.

Tommy's garden was his laboratory and, unlike those of most inventive men, it was open to public gaze. He rented a yard behind a house below the overpass that carried traffic over the CPR rails at 100 Avenue. Fifty years after Frank Oliver dismissed the whole idea of gladiolas, summer strollers could look down into a shimmer of colour travelling the spectrum from red to violet and on into white, the amalgam of all. And in many hours of the day, they would see Tommy Irvine tending his beloved gladiolas.

14

Fighting Joe Clarke:
MAYOR
FOR THE
People

IN THE HUNGRY THIRTIES, the mayors of Edmonton used to come to church suppers. In 1934, Mayor Joe Clarke came to the St. Andrew's parish supper at Westmount Community Hall. During the dessert course, he put on a demonstration that earned the admiration of all those ten years too young to vote: how to eat Jell-O with a knife.

The trembling dessert came in squares not too thick, just right for the performance. With the knife, His Worship peeled a long, thin slice from one end, then with two flicks of the wrist wrapped it around the blade, tossed it in the air, and caught it coming down—in his mouth.

Twenty years later, I would be writing about the career of Fighting Joe Clarke, Champion of the Underdog; five times mayor, eight times an alderman, every time a candidate; the youth who deserted the Mounted Police when the force failed to provide the adventure he'd expected, joining the Gold Rush crowd in the Klondike; the alderman who had a fist fight with Mayor McNamara in the council chamber; the man who used his personal friendship with Prime Minister Mackenzie King to get Edmonton a ninety-nine-year lease on the site of Commonwealth Stadium.

Those were the essential signposts on the career path of Fighting Joe Clarke, but new stories kept emerging. Clayton Thomas revealed that Joe had renounced politics forever after a humiliating defeat in Dawson City. He changed his mind, however, when he blew into Edmonton early in 1909

Joe Clarke revealing a characteristic smile.

City of Edmonton Archives CEA-10-1520

like an Ārctic chinook. He was approached immediately by boosters in the Liberal Party. Edmonton was represented in Ottawa by a Liberal icon, the Honourable Frank Oliver, minister of the interior, founder and still publisher of the *Edmonton Bulletin*. But Oliver had little interest in provincial politics. In his own constituency, the Conservatives were getting all the attention through their vociferous spokesmen, Billy McNamara and his brother Pete. Provincial Liberals were looking for a spokesman even more vociferous and recognized their man in Joe Clarke. Joe had to make some philosophical adjustments. Not only had he renounced politics forever, he had been a vociferous Conservative in the Yukon. The lure of the hustings, however, overrode these impediments. Liberal insider Stuart Darroch gave Joe a city lot to make him a property owner. Joe was off and running.

I once asked an old-time newspaperman what word he associated with Joe Clarke. With an instant chuckle he replied: "Raucous." Joe's alliance with provincial Liberals was short-lived. There weren't enough provincial elections. In the city, he could run for something every year. When he put on his show for the kids at the parish supper, he'd just been elected to his third one-year term as mayor.

Meanwhile, back at the beginning, Joe's political differences with Billy McNamara became personal, and then physical on a night in 1914 when Billy was mayor and Joe was an alderman. On August 4, the First World War broke out. On August 6, fisticuffs broke out in the council chamber and continued on the street where Joe and Billy fought to a draw (on the site of the entrance to the present-day Winspear Centre). This conflict garnered almost as much press as the one overseas. The *Bulletin* reported that Billy and Joe "intend to resign because they have so disgraced themselves and the city they can no longer hold office as elected representatives of the people."

The resignations didn't happen of course. Later, some university students went to serenade the combatants beneath their office windows. The highlight of the performance was a pantomime of two lads demonstrating the manly art of self defense. Mayor McNamara was not amused, but Joe stood in the window of his law office, exercising a raucous laugh and tossing pennies to the buskers.

Joe was never elected to the Alberta Legislature, but his raucous voice was heard there, interrupting a session with an impromptu speech from the visitor's gallery.

I have a picture in my mind of the session being interrupted. When I was in Grade Seven, my class marched three blocks from Grandin School to the Alberta Legislature to observe parliamentary government in action. From the gallery, I noted that one member was speaking, some were listening, some were taking notes, some were daydreaming, some were reading newspapers, one was doing a crossword puzzle, and one was reading the funnies.

In a quiet scene like this, I could imagine a voice booming from the gallery above...

Whatever the speaker had said, Mayor Clarke was mad as hell and wasn't going to take it anymore. There were cries for order. The sergeant-at-arms ("Damn-It-All" Turner) sent attendants scurrying up the back stairs. Before they got there, Joe had finished his unrehearsed, unrestrained, unparliamentary speech, and slipped away chuckling hugely.

In the Age of the Individual, none was more individual than Joe Clarke. The key to his character may be in the story which emerged about his grandmother. In the 1840s the potato famine was demoralizing Ireland. Margaret Marshall Clarke was the mother of seven children, living precariously on a farm in County Armagh. Margaret thought the family should make a new start in Canada, but she couldn't persuade her husband to move. She decided that at least James the baby would have hope of a better life, and took James and sailed for Ontario on her own. In 1869, James had a son named Joe. A man with such an ancestral resumé would march to no other man's drummer.

The story of the Chinese record is a glimpse into Joe's social conscience. He enjoyed music and running records on his big Victrola. He usually walked to his downtown office from his home at 7852 Jasper Avenue East, overlooking the river valley. In his first term as mayor, however (1919 to 1921), the city provided an official car with a driver. When Joe exited the car to attend a meeting somewhere, he often said to the driver: "Here's twenty bucks; go buy me some records." One day he asked the driver to find a Chinese record. The Clarkes had hired a Chinese cook, who spoke little English. The cook seemed lonely and depressed; Joe thought a Chinese record might cheer him up. Heintzmann's was able to provide one, and Joe took it home in triumph. The cook liked the record so much that it revolved from morning till night, and when the cook wasn't playing it, the Clarke children were. The process provided a certain amount of exercise. The Victrola had to be cranked for every performance. Mrs. Clarke was relieved when Joe got the cook a job in a café, and the record went with him.

The man of the people did not get off the sidewalk for the upper classes. Joe demonstrated that the day he represented the city on the visit of the governor general. Lord Willingdon seemed an agreeable chap but his Lady was, well, confrontational. The Empress Hotel in Victoria once had a portrait gallery of governor general's ladies—lush paintings and plaques with a few lines illuminating their personalities. The writer of the plaque described Lady Willingdon with exquisite tact: "Few people or events escaped her vivacious and shrewd commentary." There must have been some vivacious comments about Joe Clarke's words of welcome at the official luncheon. Joe told the crowd that Edmonton was honoured by the presence of Lord and Mrs. Willingdon. Some of Joe's fellow citizens were embarrassed that he didn't know the proper way to address the governor general's lady, but another school of thought held that Joe knew exactly what he was doing.

In the decade of severe economic and psychological depression, the people of the United States turned to an American aristocrat, Franklin Delano Roosevelt. His concern was genuine, but FDR didn't socialize with the underdog. If he knew how to eat Jell-O with his knife, he certainly wouldn't demonstrate it in a community hall, or be in a community hall in the first place. In 1932, his campaign speeches rang with elegance and inspiration. In 1934, Edmonton turned to a man of the people, who campaigned on a promise to fire the superintendent of the city's relief clothing centre. The official beat Joe to the punch, resigning on election night. Shortly after, the Champion of the Underdog came to the St. Andrew's parish supper.

Perhaps the defining story of Joe's time as mayor emerged some twenty years after in an interview with a frail lady who had memories of Edmonton from its beginnings. Names came and went; she made "vivacious commentary" about some. Inevitably, we came to Joe Clarke. There was a pause while a lovely smile gathered. Then she told a story which contained all the yearning of that time of trial. It was only seven words long: "Joe Clarke got my man a job."

15

California
DREAMING

IN THE BASEBALL SEASON OF 1922, Paul Chekolik arrived in California to pitch for the Oakland Acorns of the Pacific Coast League. He came from Edmonton, where he had grown up, gone to school, and learned the game. He was probably surprised to see his life story in the sport pages, surprised at how it had been rewritten by the team's publicity man. The folks back home, including his fans at Diamond Park, would have been more surprised still, reading the saga of...

CHEKOLIK THE ESKIMO

Through a howling blizzard, an Eskimo lad approached the Canadian trading post of Fort Vermilion. He had to lean against the blizzard. Men could get lost only ten feet from each other, but Chekolik was determined to reach this outpost of civilization and better himself.

At Fort Vermilion he worked for the fur traders and learned about the town of Edmonton, many hundreds of miles to the south. He was filled with a new determination to see Edmonton. He found that in Edmonton the ground was free of snow for three months of the year, and the game of baseball was played occasionally. He quickly mastered the fundamentals of the game and attracted the attention of a baseball scout named "Deacon" White. That started Paul Chekolik on a career in baseball.

Source: *Oakland Tribune*, 1922

This press agent's whimsy was no more inaccurate than Hollywood biographies of famous composers, but it sold tickets. Oakland fans would look up from their morning papers and exclaim: "Chekolik the Eskimo is pitching today. Take me out to the ball game!"

16

THE
BREWER'S
Tale

THERE WAS A BUZZ around Edmonton's City Centre Airport on a fall day in 1945. The famous Captain Crownover had landed his U.S. Army transport plane with a secret cargo bound for a secret destination. Though the war was over, Blatchford Field was still one of the busiest military aviation scenes in North America, with an American base along the east side (now occupied by NAIT).

The name Joseph C. Crownover was not familiar to the public, but he was a celebrity in the world of aviation, where news travelled at the speed of flight. In August he'd been the first American to land in Japan, days after the second atomic bomb, the war not yet officially over. At his headquarters in Manila, General MacArthur was preparing to lead an army of occupation into Japan and wondered what sort of reception his troops would get. Captain Crownover was sent to find out.

Crownover's mission was simple. He was to fly to Tokyo, land at the main airport, and see what happened. At the airport nothing happened. Officials were courteous, and that was a relief. Now, Captain Crownover and his two crewmen had to test the reaction of the civilian population to the sight of American men in uniform walking the streets of Tokyo. They ventured into the city with uncomfortable thoughts of going down in history as the last casualties of the Pacific War. The people were curious, sometimes loudly, but courteous. Captain Crownover flew back to Manila with good news for the general.

Some weeks later, when Crownover dropped out of the wild blue yonder into Edmonton, people at the air base knew who he was. And when the buzz got around that the first pilot to land in Japan was entrusted with a secret cargo bound for an unknown destination—they agreed that the cargo must be something of grave significance. Crownover waited here more than a week for his next orders, and took off pointing north. He was back in a few days with the secret of the cargo. It was beer. Three thousand cans of beer.

There is a moral to this story—if *moral* is defined as "a lesson contained in a fable, a story or an event." The Crownover case teaches that beer has a history in Edmonton, and more than history, a tradition older than community leagues, medical breakthroughs, champion teams, bush pilots, oil wells, or festivals. And beer is the only Edmonton tradition to be upheld by the Supreme Court of Canada.

Beer reached the highest legal plateau in the 1950s when Bohemian Maid sought to expand its brewery on Saskatchewan Drive. The brewery was almost invisible, on the north side of the drive, about 106 Street. All that showed was the proverbial tip of the iceberg, a modest one-storey office block. And on the lawn in front stood a curious concrete statue of a small bear on its hind legs, beloved of children. Out of sight, straggling down the hillside, concrete bunkers contained tanks, vats, and pipes. It gave Edmonton the distinction of the only city in North America with a brewery in the middle of a public park; a distinction civic authorities could do without. So when the brewery wanted to expand, the city took its objections to court. In the end, the highest court ruled that the brewery was there first and therefore had the right to stay and to expand on the site where brewing began. There was once a spring on the hillside, emerging clear and bright from the poplars, ferns, and broad-leaf creepers, a sight to stir the soul of a poet, or a man who had come all the way from Germany (by way of Chicago) to make beer.

Robert Oschner landed in Chicago at eighteen, in the centre of a continent where fellow émigrés like Pabst, Schlitz, Busch, Hamm, Anheuser, and Budweiser were making names for themselves on beer bottles. He decided he would add Oschner to the list. He arrived in Strathcona in 1894 and began brewing, with the help of the spring and his young wife. He was the manager and salesman; she was our first and only lady brewmaster.

They built their brewery with lumber that John Walter gave them on credit and went to work, a prodigious amount of work, converting the spring to brew. Mrs. Oschner was slight and pale with blonde hair brushed straight back. Mr. Oschner was a perfect barrel of a man with a blonde moustache and bright pink complexion fairly shouting the benefits of Oschner's beer. He was a solid citizen, literally and figuratively, excited by the celebrations of 1899 when Strathcona obtained its town charter. He liked the decorations on Whyte Avenue: "Der town vass all lit oop...mit leckrish lights und everyding." The family brew sold so well that when the Oschners wearied of leckrish lights and other icons of urban living, he traded his interest in the *Strathcona* Brewing and Malting Company for three thousand acres of ranchland near Bittern Lake, leaving a modern plant on the site of the woodland spring.

Oschner had competition from Tom Cairns, who also arrived here in 1894 to found the *Edmonton* Brewing and Malting Company. While Oschner was making beer out of spring water, Cairns was making it out of the river. He'd learned the art in Portage la Prairie. When two breweries in a row burned down around him, he decided there must be better luck in Edmonton. In partnership with Kelly and Myover, Cairns built a small plant in Rossdale, just upstream from the present Low Level Bridge, and made foaming brew from the river that flowed past his door. Whenever the river got too muddy and fragrant for the purpose, he had a well beside the plant. Cairns's product went well but relations with his partners did not. After four years, he pulled out and with help from John Walter built another brewery upstream, where the Royal Glenora Club presides today. Cairns malted and brewed for the Gold Rush crowd, then in 1900 took the Klondike trail himself, with an offer to run a brewery in Dawson City. The "Royal Glenora" plant was abandoned, but the brewhouse remained for half a century as the roothouse of a Chinese market garden.

But that wasn't the end of the *Edmonton* Brewing and Malting Company. The owner of the Strathcona Hotel saw opportunity in Tom's dormant enterprise. W. H. Sheppard bought beer and sold it. It seemed reasonable that he could make it as well. So he acquired Tom's equipment, his original site by the Low Level Bridge, and built a highly-visible red-brick fortress for brewing. In 1904, this gave him the most strategic location to distribute the product. The big brewery horses fanned out northward delivering kegs as far away as St. Albert. Looking the other direction, his brewery was on the only bit of railway track north of the river, the last gasp of the Edmonton Yukon and Pacific. Freight cars with the product could connect through Mill Creek to towns on the Calgary and Edmonton Railway, the only line to the south. Beer went out on the railway on many days, but never on Sunday; that was the law. Then an Edmonton Yukon and Pacific dispatcher sensed a loophole in the law. It was all right to dispatch perishable goods; the more he thought about it, beer was perishable. Away went the train, but someone was watching. The dispatcher was summoned to court. His rationale was a good try, but not good enough.

Perhaps some neighbours didn't appreciate a brewery in their midst, but Leon Von Schlembrook did. Leon came from Belgium with a group of coal miners who settled in Rossdale to work at the Star Mine and start market gardens. Leon liked vegetables of course, but he loved beer. He showed his affection in the way he said the word—not a clipped flat *beer*, but a lingering *beeee—urr*, almost a whisper, like the benediction of an indulgent providence on the human race. Leon's mystical reverence for beer made him a welcome visitor at the brewery. Spectators wondered at the coat he wore for those occasions. It was old, tattered, and several sizes too generous for his frame, but held a secret—a secret lining. Leon would go clink-clink-clink all the way home, and in the evening would "set them up" for his Belgian friends. Years passed. Leon and his friends did well with their gardens and moved up out of the valley to commercial operations; Leon went to Bremner. Prohibition came and went; beer parlours replaced bars. When Leon felt that his time was growing short, he arranged a happy funeral. After his friends accompanied him on his last ride, they made for their favourite beer parlour where the terms of Leon Von Schlembrook's last will and testament would "set them up." When they got there, however, the true mourning began. It was Election Day. The beer parlour was closed!

In 1904, Mr. Sheppard's brewery in Rossdale had a prime strategic location. But the tsunami of the first Edmonton boom was about to burst over the landscape. Soon, railroads were all over the place. The Canadian Pacific built into Strathcona from the east, then built the High Level Bridge to carry its track into Edmonton city centre. The brewery was left down in the valley at the end of a stub track going one direction only. The population was exploding—to perhaps ten times what it was in 1904—and the newcomers were 150 feet above the valley, a gruelling climb for Sheppard's big horses. In nine years, the brewery's position went from strategic to tragic. In 1913, he moved out of the valley to the west end, to a new red-brick plant with a sort of Gothic tower at 121 Street and 105 Avenue. From this location, Mr. Sheppard would advertise that the plant was on no less than five railways and, therefore, could assure quickest delivery of the high-quality product to all points in northern Alberta.

The owners were happy with the new address, which also made for contented pigs on farms along the St. Albert Trail. When beer was poured off the brewing kettles, a sweet sludge remained at the bottom, a compound of grain, malt, and a few percentage points of alcohol. Wagons bound for the farms trailed a sweet smell in their wake. The cargo was nutritious for pigs and apparently fit for human consumption as well. Kids, who observe everything, noted the teamsters digging into it.

In 1916, an historic social groundswell jolted the brewing industry. The men of Alberta voted for prohibition. Women were prime movers in the cause but did not yet have the vote. Production and sale of hard liquor was banned. Beer was limited to two-percent alcohol. This put brewers in a never-never land. Consumers would never concede that the stuff was worthy of the name. Bob Edwards once treated readers of the *Calgary Eye-Opener* to a spoof about the man who invented two-percent beer paying for his crime on the gallows at Fort Saskatchewan. Oschner's plant on Saskatchewan Drive went dark.

Ironically, the Edmonton Brewing and Malting Company could still produce the beer that had made its reputation, but only for export to other provinces. In 1921, this situation got to be too much for Morris (Two-Gun)

Cohen and his fellow veterans at the Memorial Hall (where Telus Tower stands now). The Prince of Wales was coming to town. His Royal Highness would be hobnobbing with the swells but would also be entertained at the Legion. The boys couldn't insult their future king by offering him two-percent muck. The government conceded the point, and after the popular prince went on his way, the Memorial Hall remained an oasis in a desert of two-percent beer—till 1923, when Alberta abandoned the attempt to prohibit liquor in favour of liquor control.

Repeal restored the fortunes of the brewery on 121 Street and revived the existence of the one on Saskatchewan Drive. The Bank of Montreal had become reluctant owners by default and didn't consider this asset valuable enough to keep a watchman on it. Doors had disappeared. Pigeons flew in and out the broken windows. Kids played cops and robbers among the echoing ruins. Then early in 1923, W.L. Wilkin (real estate, insurance, and investment broker known to his friends as Billy) caught a whiff of a hint that the government might be thinking about a plebiscite to see if Albertans had given up on prohibition. Billy and twenty-four friends moved softly and swiftly. They each put in a hundred dollars and offered it to the bank for a six-month option to purchase the plant. In November, a referendum confirmed their status as shrewd investors. Our first brewery came to new life for a half century in which it would make consumer history with the popular Bohemian Maid label, and legal history when the Supreme Court of Canada ruled that a brewery can stay in a public park if it was there first.

The second age was brought to an end in 1976, when a larger competitor bought the plant for the purpose of shutting it down. The office block and the beloved bear disappeared, but down the hillside the concrete bunkers of the brewhouse remained massively intact—an ideal facility for the City Artifacts Centre. Objects of all facets of Edmonton's history are preserved where the history of brewing began.

On the north side, Sheppard's brewery pumped beer till 2007, when the company shifted all its bottling operations to the Maritimes. The future of the building is clouded, but down in Rossdale, Mr. Sheppard's brick fortress, beloved of Leon Von Schlembrook, stands sturdy as ever in its second century. Architect Gene Dub has remodelled it as a residence. Cheers!

THE
MAN
== IN THE ==
White Vest

J.H. PICARD WAS NEVER THE MAN TO RUSH INTO THINGS. He was born in Quebec City in 1867, into an era when young men going west did so at twenty or younger. He waited till he was thirty and went as far as Qu'Appelle, Saskatchewan. At thirty-five, he was on the move again, following the new Calgary and Edmonton Railway to see if his fortune lay somewhere along the track. His quest took him right to the end of the line. He arrived in Edmonton in 1892 and formed a friendship and partnership with a fellow-Francophone, Stanislaus "Sandy" Larue. Larue and Picard opened a general store on Jasper Avenue (on the site of Macdonald Place) and had trading posts in northern Alberta.

Inevitably, there were land deals. J.H. Picard made one that is a legend in the chronicles of Edmonton real estate. He acquired a corner of Jasper Avenue at 104 Street—the northeast corner where the Birks Building is—in a trade with Georges Roy, Edmonton's first civil servant. The legend offers three versions of what Picard surrendered to get it. Was it an alpaca coat? Was it a pair of pants? Was it a coat and vest without the pants? Whichever version is closest to fact, both men were content with their bargain.

While Picard had thought long and hard before going west, he thought longer and harder about getting married. He didn't take that step until he was forty-six. His friends were so pleased that they gave him a bachelor party that must have set some sort of record. They drank to the future happiness of their friend and his bride, Martine Voyer, with three thousand dollars worth of champagne.

This is a classic street scene in Edmonton in the 1890s: two men standing in the middle of the street, enjoying a leisurely chat. The street is Jasper Avenue, with Ross Brothers Hardware on the left (now Canada Place), and the *Bulletin* newspaper office on the right (now Shaw Conference Centre). There's a sagging pole in the street, holding up the wires of the telephone system. The pole is not a threat to traffic and traffic not to it. No horse-drawn vehicle is in sight. The only animal is the dog standing with the men. The man on the right is Richard Secord of McDougall

and Secord, traders and financiers (as identified by his son Dick Junior). The man in the white vest is Joseph Henri Picard (as identified by his son Laurier). The white vest was a fashion statement from Paris. J. H. Picard was the only man in Edmonton who had all his suits tailored in Paris. His sense of what was right extended to his overcoats, of which he had three. The raccoon was for every day, the beaver for Sunday, and the Persian lamb for special occasions.

Picard was delighted when their home was blessed with a baby boy but was puzzled that Madame insisted he be named Ro-bair (Robert). He protested that no one in either family was ever Ro-bair, but Madame would hear of nothing else. After Father Lemarchand baptized the child, Madame revealed her secret. She had named the first-born in honour of her political hero Sir Robert Borden, leader of the Conservative Party of Canada. Madame didn't have a vote, but she had undoubtedly scored one for the Conservatives. The joke went around the town. Her Liberal husband agreed that it was a fine joke, but the next son would be Laurier for his hero, Sir Wilfrid, the prime minister.

Ro-bair became a Jesuit priest and prominent educator in Montreal. Laurier became a popular figure in Edmonton's theatre community with his flair for light comedy, and he was a high school drama teacher in the Catholic school board. J. H. Picard was a member of that board for twenty-five years, chairman for fifteen. He was on the Edmonton town council and eventually the city council. He was modest about his contribution to these bodies. A friend once asked him what he did at all those meetings. "Oh," he shrugged, "sometime second da moshe, sometime move adjourn."

He tried to extend modesty to anonymity in a happening that might be called The Affair of the Sanctuary Carpet. The carpet around the altar of his church, St. Joachim's, was noticeably tattered and worn. The small "Christmas Card" church (still standing at 110 Street near 100 Avenue) was big enough then for all the Catholics in town, with one mass in French and another in English. One day, a salesman for a Belgian carpetmaker came into Picard's store. Picard fingered the rich samples and thought of the threadbare rug in the church. Then he had another thought. "Ha!" he told the agent, "you come wid me." Like conspirators, they made a fast trip to St. Joachim's, took measurements of the sanctuary, and got away unobserved.

Picard then ordered the finest carpet the salesman offered. It would have to come from Brussels which would take time, but that would be time for Picard to anticipate and enjoy the sensation it would cause. It arrived on a Saturday—not an ordinary Saturday, but the eve of Easter Sunday. Picard made for the church with the surprise he'd bought for the congregation. The church was empty. He planned to lay the carpet and leave without anyone seeing him.

Picard was half finished putting down the carpet when Father Lemarchand walked in. He saw amazement and alarm in the pastor's face and understood the alarm. "It is all right, Père. It will cost you nothing. I make it a free gift...on the condition that my name be not mentioned."

Father Lemarchand agreed and was as good as his word. After the English mass next morning, he announced: "You 'ave notice we 'ave a new carpet in da sanctuary. Beautiful new carpet but don't you worry. Won't cost you nothing, it is a gift. Alas, I cannot reveal the name of the person who donated it. I can only tell you that he is in business with Mr. Larue."

18

WHEN

Old Strathcona

— WAS —

YOUNG

IN THE 1950S, when we lived in King Edward Park, we had wonderful neighbours next door, a kindly older couple, Minna and Fred Garbe. Fred was an Old Strathcona original. His time to be young was the first dozen years or so of the century, and he had the stories to prove it.

Fred was a resourceful chap with talented hands. He built much of his house himself. During the Depression, he and some pals went to the Klondike and sluiced a living from recycling gravel from old Gold Rush claims. In the Second World War, he worked at the airport. He had a resourceful souvenir of that experience: a heavy wheelbarrow crafted from scraps of wood, tin, and iron. He also had a certifiable historical artifact, a tailwheel from one of the many DC-3 military transports which passed through Edmonton back then. We fell heir to the wheelbarrow, and it served us for many years. Though it is no longer fit for service, it remains as a unique lawn ornament, a reminder of Fred Garbe and the stories he told about Old Strathcona. For which, please read on.

While there's no dispute that winters were worse long ago, it's equally true that summers were better, and nowhere better than in the Golden Age of Old Strathcona. This was the time before Strathcona lost its independence through amalgamation (1912) and its position as terminus of the Edmonton and Calgary Railway through the High Level Bridge (1913).

The Golden Age was Fred Garbe's time to be young, when kids were really free in summer, free of school, free of organized activities, free of adults ensuring their safety. Fred and his companions were free to dam Mill Creek without notice to, or by, officialdom. In the 1950s, the city of Edmonton built a swimming pool *on* Mill Creek, but back in Fred's time, the kids built one *in* the creek at 76 Avenue, and they did so every year because the floods of spring carried off the last summer's dam. As soon as the creek slowed down, the kids would gather logs and rocks. They'd raise a dam about five feet high and thirty feet wide. While it would be something less than watertight, it would hold back enough to form a curving pool 150 yards long and, in places, six feet deep. All summer, the stream ran full, out of the forest primeval. Rainfall gravitating towards the creek was not intercepted by storm sewers.

That was the life, floating downstream with the current...the high green bank on the west just a few feet away...the whistle of the Edmonton Yukon and Pacific engine shunting cattle cars down to Gainer's packing plant...the sun moving lazily across the high vault of heaven...till the sound of rushing water grew louder and your head was bobbing against the timbers of the dam...time to swim upstream and float back again.

But life was not all play. In the good old summertime of 1907, Strathcona created business opportunities for enterprising lads. The town was about to acquire the charter of a city and, in keeping with its heightened dignity, passed a "herd law." Contented cows grazing at will along city streets and lanes were poor expressions of the new status. It would be legal for a family to keep a cow, but she must stay on the property. This was a problem. Few cows could find enough to eat in their own backyards, so enterprising lads were hired to take them to the free green pastures which later became a campus for the University of Alberta. The going wage was a dollar-and-a-half per cow per month. A lad like Fred Garbe could also increase his income by picking the wild raspberries. He could pick fifty to sixty quarts in a season, and sell them door-to-door for two cents a quart.

There was a downside to sunlit days with the cows. The herder could miss some excitement on Whyte Avenue. An arithmetic book of the time might have explained it in these terms: "If A has five dollars which says his horse can beat B's horse, and B has ten dollars which says his horse can beat A's horse, and B's horse loses, how many dollars does A have?" The answer would be found in a public contest on Whyte Avenue.

Money was bet freely on high-speed horses but even more changed hands over the predicted capabilities of the heavy-duty breeds. There was always a gang around the station when a train came in. The gang would look over the heavy machinery sitting on the flatcars—such as boilers and engines—and make bets on whether the horses present had the muscle to haul these things to their destinations.

A record was set the day the town brought in the boilers for the Strathcona power plant, which sat on the river across from the present EPCOR plant. The boilers were huge. There were bets on whether they could be manhandled onto the drays. Then there were bets on whether the horses could drag them to the top of Old Fort Road. The horses made winners of those who believed in their hauling power. At the top of Old Fort Road, however, the betting became more complicated. There was no doubt the boilers would go down the hill. The question was: Would they get there ahead of the horses? To the relief of all, even those who had bet against them, the horses won.

The horses won another epic pull, which became a legend because of an incident at the successful finish. It began when the Dominion Hotel bought a big safe to store the liquor. Since the safe was bought from a business on just the other side of Whyte Avenue, the movers decided they would not struggle to load and unload a dray for the 100-foot journey. Their horses would drag the monster across on its reinforced-steel bottom. It would do the dirt road no harm. A knowledgeable crowd gathered, making bets on whether two horses were enough for the job. This body of experts attracted an even larger crowd of the merely curious. The contest was on—two strong horses versus the safe.

There were many starts, every few feet, as the horses mustered irresistible force to pull the immovable object. The horses drew closer...and closer...to the finish. The battle was won...and then...it happened. One horse slipped on a round stone. The stone flew, as did the horse. His fierce straining energy translated into a cartwheel. His harness broke. He crashed into the front of the hotel in a shower of plate glass. The hotel manager was not upset. He'd won his bet, which was the important thing. He dived through the space that used to be a window to attend to the horse. Despite the confusion of finding himself in the lobby of the Dominion Hotel, the gallant horse was fine. He emerged to an ovation.

Then there was the story Paul Theriault used to tell. Paul was a jovial Francophone and a droll master of telling a story on himself. He told this one often, by request. Fred Garbe said people would laugh till they were sick. The basic plot turns up as folklore in a number of places. It couldn't have happened in all of them, but must have happened somewhere—where better than here?

Paul had run a livery stable on Whyte Avenue when the horse held a monopoly on transportation. One day, he loaded his family onto a wagon and drove off to a farm near Leduc. He was often in town and became intrigued by the noisy machines that Henry Ford had loosed on the world. On one trip, he became so heavily intrigued that he traded his horse and wagon for a Model-T. Amid shouts and cheers, the boys showed him how to steer. They cranked the engine to life, and he rattled away to disturb the silence of the trail home.

When he appeared next on Whyte Avenue, he came driving a horse and wagon, which raised the inevitable question: "Where's the Model-T?" The answer was a performance he would encore many times. Radiating boisterous good humour, he would take the audience along on that first drive. How exciting it was to go pounding along the trail as familiar sights went tumbling past at the unfamiliar rate of twelve miles an hour. How he laughed to hear the engine's four throbbing cylinders fire a steady kak-kak-kak-kak-kak-kak-kak into the passing woods. How people laughed and waved as he clattered past. How surprised they were. And how surprised his family would be. How they would exclaim when he drove into the yard and stopped triumphantly by the house. (A pause. Paul's broad face would contort into a massive frown, his dark eyes rolled towards heaven.) When he stopped! Oh! No one had told him how to stop. He should have asked. Too late now. The farmhouse was in view. With luck, the gate would be open; he would have time to think. But it wasn't. Pieces of gate flew off in all directions along with the barnyard birds. People were running out of the house and right back in again as the Model-T bore down on them. Paul steered a wide circle around the house and then another as the livestock retreated to a prudent distance. In need of time to think over his situation, Paul headed out across the fields. Still trying to think, he approached the house again and family who had come outside ran back in again. He circled the house and went out in the field again, surprised at how fast the pig ahead of him could run. He steered around a haystack, went a hundred yards past, and turned back. The haystack was the answer to his prayer.

He took it head-on. Straw erupted all about him but he'd found a way to stop the car. (He held up a cautionary hand. There was more.) The impact had ruptured the fuel tank. Gas was running out. The straw was on fire. The Model-T was on fire. The haystack and its contents went up in smoke.

But there was a happy ending after all. Paul Theriault had survived to tell the tale. Many times.

19

LAUGHING OFF THE

Northwest
REBELLION

ON A DAY IN THE DARK COLD SPRING of 1885, a Native named Grasshopper came to the kitchen door of Frank Oliver. Grasshopper was a handyman who did odd jobs for Mrs. Oliver. On this day, Grasshopper was not his amiable self. He stood sullen and silent—till he pointed to a pie she had cooling. "Give me some of that pie." He took it, glared at it, took it to the door, and threw it on the ground. "That is what I think of your pie."

Mrs. Oliver was surprised but not flustered, thinking that Grasshopper was having the 1885 equivalent of a bad day. But there was more to it. Unrest from the Métis uprising in Saskatchewan had spread to First Nations around Edmonton. They were converging from all sides, pitching their lodges on the present Victoria Golf Course. Within days, families taking refuge in Fort Edmonton saw the campfires and heard drums at night. In this test of pioneer spirit, Frank Oliver's newspaper decided that fear should be put into perspective with humour. On April 4, the *Bulletin* reported: "Edmonton, for a wonder, has at last got excited about something."

Rumours were fanning the excitement. On March 31, the telegraph line went dead, cut by Riel's men somewhere in Saskatchewan. Edmonton was isolated. The telegraph was the town's—and the newspaper's—only link to the outside world. In lieu of news, rumours filled the void, rumours of everything including massacres. The Edmonton Volunteer Infantry, a home guard formed in two days, were busy on the grounds of today's Alberta Legislature, transforming the Hudson's Bay fur trade fort into a military fortress. The big concern was attack with flaming arrows. Seventeen years before, angry Blackfeet camped in Kinsmen Park, shot burning arrows over the river into the fort, and burned down the stockade. In 1885, the Volunteer Infantry dug a well inside the fort, and they brought in a portable steam engine to power the hoses.

In this abnormal situation, Frank Oliver's paper assured readers that the institutions of the town, with a population (arguably) of five hundred, were functioning normally. Members of the Cemetery Society, for example, were showing grace under pressure. They continued regular weekly meetings, a message to all that they expected to arrive at the cemetery in the fullness of their allotted years.

The Literary Society was also showing calm. There was a full turnout for the April meeting to hear a debate on the topic: Resolved that the works of nature are more beautiful than works of art. The society ruled that nature has it over art, with the clinching argument advanced by Tommy Lauder, the volunteer fire chief. Tommy said he would rather look at a pretty girl than a picture of the same, no matter how skilful the artist. Having put art in its place, the society voted with a show of hands, and a show of optimism, to meet in May to debate whether the farmer is more independent than the mechanic.

The *Bulletin's* editorial position was: "Everybody stay calm." The publisher and his family set an example. They did not seek shelter of the fort. They were visibly at home. Frank was seen preparing his patch of prairie for summer. There were alarms, of course, and the *Bulletin* was pleased to report one which illustrated President Roosevelt's advice about the Great Depression: "We have nothing to fear but fear itself." A perceived menace turned out to be only a couple of the Ancient and Honourable Order of Calithumpians in full tribal regalia." At a distance, fear transformed two whooping Scots in Highland costume into a party of hostile Natives.

As more campfires were counted on the golf course each night, ideas were hatching for defense of the settlement. One such idea led to the Great Whiskey Raid. It occurred to some concerned citizens that a number of illegal stills were bubbling in the woods beyond the town, and it would be a bad thing if the Natives should get into the stills. Some of the stuff would make a saint want to go to war. So, one night they commandeered two wagons and went off into the woods on a pre-emptive strike. Most of the product was dumped on the ground, but some…well, some was so smooth, so close to maturity that they couldn't bear to treat it like that. So they returned, banging dishpans and singing lustily to let the town know they were the heroes from the Great Whiskey Raid. They rode round and round the few streets, spreading the good news until (as the *Bulletin* reported) "on an impulse they dismounted and trooped into Kelly's saloon, much to the public relief."

In the second week of the siege, a difference of opinion broke out over defense strategy. Majority opinion held that all available defense should be concentrated on the refuge of the fort. The town was a mile away, clustered around the present site of Canada Place. It was best to abandon the town, board up the buildings, and hope they wouldn't be torched. If that happened, well, it was only property; lives were more important than property.

Men who owned these buildings did not disagree that lives were more important but felt strongly that property was entitled to some respect too. Three leading men of property met in Kelly's saloon and constituted themselves a Committee for the General Defense: John Brown, the man with the biggest general store; Ed Carey, the free trader; and D. R. Fraser, the lumberman. There were five stores containing merchandise to the value of $50,000. They would defend these and other properties against all comers. To show their resolve, they would construct their own downtown fort.

The committee moved swiftly with an ingenious plan. On the morning of April 11, twenty-five men chopped away trees from a strip of land along the north rim of the town. The clearing would give two benefits. It would deprive hostiles of cover for surveillance or attack, and it would produce a pile of logs for the fort. By four o'clock, the committee was ready to start construction. At that point, however, the project died. Word came from the Mounted Police that they were sending thirty troopers from Fort Saskatchewan; all were assigned to the defense of old Fort Edmonton.

This news fractured the committee. John Brown, whose store was just behind the proposed fort, thought they should press on. Ed Carey, whose store happened to be up west near Fort Edmonton, thought they should abandon the project. D.R. Fraser, whose mill was down in Riverdale, and not likely to benefit much from either fort, thought they should help out at Fort Edmonton. With the committee divided against itself, the twenty-five workmen decided to give up and go home.

Day after day, nothing happened. There were some alarms, but nothing happened. Belief grew that troops from eastern Canada must be on the way. On May 1, there they were, on the high bank across the river—the 65th Mount Royal Rifles, all the way from Quebec. They lifted the siege, and the cloud which hung over Edmonton's spring of 1885. Life and business returned to normal. The quartermaster of the 65th would attest to that. He was soon writing his superiors that if the merchants of Edmonton were to charge Riel and the rebels the way they were charging *him*, the conflict would not last long.

And it was business as usual for Grasshopper. He was back doing odd jobs for Mrs. Oliver.

20

HOW'S
Reg Lister?

WHEN DR. WALTER JOHNS WAS PRESIDENT of the University of Alberta, he enjoyed the alumnae tours. In the years 1969 to 1974, he went from sea to sea telling graduates of the current achievements of their university. He would then ask for questions, and he knew what the first question would be.

If Dr. Johns were to tell them that their university had produced three Nobel Prize winners, had found a cure for the common cold, had established how many angels could dance on the head of a pin, and been ranked number one by *Maclean's* magazine, the first question would always be: "How's Reg Lister?"

Though Reg Lister was never a student or professor, upon his retirement as senior employee of the university, he received the tribute of two generations of students at the spring convocation in 1949. He was declared an honorary graduate.

Reg was there before the students and knew the campus literally from the ground up. His first job was digging a basement for the home of President Henry Marshall Tory. Reg came from England in 1911, from the quiet borough of Hingham, Norfolk, best known as the birthplace of Abraham Lincoln's grandfather. He arrived in Edmonton in time to watch the coronation parade for King George V and Queen Mary. In the crowd, he was greeted by two young neighbours from Hingham. The Kerby brothers were working on the new campus. They took twenty-year-old Reg to meet the foreman, and he was handed a shovel and directed to dig a foundation for Ring House 1.

Reg Lister's Campus, seen from the air in 1928. Clockwise from top left are the student residences—Pembina Hall, Assiniboia Hall, and Athabasca Hall where Reg lived for half a century as caretaker and student counsellor; St. Joseph's College; the Medical Building with Convocation Hall behind; St. Stephen's College facing the beloved Varsity Tuck Shop across 112 Street; the University Hospital; the hospital vegetable gardens and the Varsity Covered Rink, one of three in the city. At the top of 112 Street, just to the right, sits Rutherford House.

When he walked to the dig in the early morning, he would often see deer running in the poplar woods. A little later, the mules would arrive for the heavy duty. The air would turn blue as mule-skinners instructed the critters in the only language mules understand.

Reg saw the campus happen. He watched the mules drag out a basement for Athabasca Hall, the first major building. Then he counted every brick delivered to the site. The contractor was determined to have every brick he'd paid for. When the hall was finished, Reg moved in—as caretaker. It was his home for half the century.

Assiniboia Hall came next. Reg was watching when the mules hauled two mighty boulders out of the excavation. These souvenirs of the last ice age became campus icons, sacred to the memory of undergraduate romances, relaxing places to sit and talk, showing no sign of wear in a hundred years. Reg could be a willing accessory if he approved of a match. Before the First World War, he carried secret notes to Miss Carmichael, the registrar's secretary, from future Chief Justice Bill Howson. Summer school was a particularly busy time for boy-meets-girl. Teachers came from the country for professional advancement and other considerations. Summer school was known as Fred McNally's Matrimonial Bureau. McNally was the deputy minister of education.

This activity was subject to extreme decorum, as were all things on campus, though dances were now permitted. Dr. Tory had given up his attempt to replace the dance with the conversazione. He believed sincerely that dancing was improper and offered a compromise in which couples could link hands and promenade around the room to music while making conversazione. After a brave battle with the inevitable, the first president accepted defeat. He also relented on the matter of students wearing academic gowns to class. Men were required, however, to attend in suits and ties.

There were student demonstrations then, though not motivated by ideology. Reg witnessed a typical show in 1913 when Dr. Tory's charges rearranged the program for the official opening of the traffic deck on the High Level Bridge. The day before it was to be handed over by the contractor, a lively crowd took down the barriers at the south end and marched across, led by Sandy Carmichael on a donkey. The sole motivation was highjinks, a quaint notion defined as "mischievous merriment."

If the proverbial man-on-the-street were to be asked what words came to mind when he heard the expression "college boy," he would likely shout, "Rah, Rah!" Sons of parents who could pay for higher education were allowed three years of petty lunacy. It was accepted, almost expected, of lads like the pair who tied a toboggan to the back of a streetcar for a thrill ride across the top deck of the High Level. They were having a whale of a time—another 1913ism—till the trolley accelerated. Their toboggan swung from side to side, held in by the rails. When it swung to the outside, they had a horrifying look into space—and into eternity. Luck bailed them out, as it usually did. When the toboggan swung to the inside, they rolled off and crept to safety on the train track…with a tale to tell back in Athabasca Hall.

Engineers incorporated technology into highjinks. One morning after Halloween, Reg joined a crowd by St. Stephen's College to look up at Dr. Tory's buggy swinging from a third-floor turret. In 1919 Wop May, the wartime ace, was very briefly an engineering student. He and his classmates borrowed a cannon from the Connaught Armoury (today, a succession of failed nightclubs) and spent an evening firing blanks they'd made up in the lab. Reg was fond of the Dickson twins from Medicine Hat, even though Johnny caught gophers and made pets of them, and Charlie found mischievous merriment shooting out streetlights from his window.

A future governor general of Canada performed some minor vandalism on Athabasca Hall. In 1958, when the culprit was Speaker of the House of Commons, Reg could still point out his name, carved into the window frame of Room 218: Rollie Michener.

Reg accepted the student highjinks. More than accepting, he understood. He also understood their troubles and hopes and fears. And the students sensed it. When he retired after thirty-eight years, they tried to find words to express the contribution this modest caretaker had made to their lives: "Mr. Lister, though not a member of the academic staff of the University, has taught the students some of the most important things they learned there."

A list of important things was not attached. Perhaps there were no specifics. Perhaps it was a matter of learning what things are important. Perhaps it was just the art of living.

Whatever it was, when Dr. Walter Johns was routinely asked: "How's Reg Lister?" it wouldn't have occurred to the questioner that Reg might have died. He wasn't the type for it. He seemed as timeless and permanent as the romantic rocks in front of Athabasca Hall. But he had passed on in 1960, short of the Biblical allotment of three score and ten. The university had bestowed a posthumous honour on the honorary graduate: a massive student residence—a complex with twin towers—Lister Hall.

21

IRISH
Occasions

THE SEVENTEENTH OF OLD IRELAND was a civic holiday in Edmonton—for one time only. This Irish occasion brightened the spring of 1904, brought on by men who understood the significance of St. Patrick's Day not only to the Irish but to the town which was about to claim the stature of a city, and a capital city to boot. Bob Smith was a red-haired auctioneer; Tommy Irvine was an innovator in many areas. They thought business should cease to trouble for a full observance of the day. They circulated a petition through the business community, and the only man who turned them down was Johnstone Walker. Despite this Irish relations gaffe, the department store he founded was able to survive for ninety-seven years.

There was a parade of course. It marshalled in Rossdale, on the racetrack where Sir Wilfrid Laurier would come the next year to inaugurate the province. The Strathcona Town Band came across the river to lead the parade, and the bandsmen needed all their wind and stamina. It was not the longest parade in local history, but it may have had the longest parade *route*— up the steep grade of 97 Avenue to 109 Street, north to Jasper Avenue, east along Jasper Avenue to 97 Street, then west on 102 Avenue to 108 Street.

In his decorated carriage, "Professor" Jones the barber demonstrated the universality of St. Patrick's Day. "Professor" Jones was a black man and a member of the Orange Lodge.

In the evening, the occasion became a concert at Robertson's Hall. It was an artistic and financial success, raising 150 dollars for Edmonton hospitals. Is it mere coincidence that for much of the twentieth century the hospitals of Old Ireland were financed by a worldwide lottery, the Irish Sweepstakes? In Canada, this fundraiser was aided by a quirk in the law which has something Irish about it. While it was illegal to sell sweepstake tickets, it was all right to buy them.

November 24, 1952 saw another Irish occasion at the Canadian National Railway station. Police Chief Reg Jennings welcomed twenty-five Irishmen, recent members of the Royal Ulster constabulary, recruited to help his force deal with a population growing past 200,000. On a morning shortly after, the chief announced that the Irish cops would be out on the streets that day, walking beats in pairs, to meet the people. In the newsroom at CJCA, we had just acquired a portable tape recorder, the latest technology in radio news operations. From the fourth floor of the Birks Building, we went down onto Jasper Avenue to seek Irish accents for the recorder. In minutes, there approached an average-size Irish policeman in step with a very large one who was extending a smile broad enough to reach the far side of the avenue. The tall officer was the obvious spokesman for the patrol. People who tuned into our noonday news (sponsored by McGavin's Bakery) heard the voice of a leprechaun with the darting mischievous wit of those legendary sprites.

This lively sound bite gave notice that Sam Donaghey would be heard from again...as on the Irish occasion when Sam was made a member of the Order of Canada...and the six multicultural occasions when Sam was made honorary chief of a Native band. He was the biggest blue-eyed chief at all public ceremonies in Edmonton. People were amused by the towering, smiling presence, in the feather headdress, because they didn't understand the honour. Here's the story: When Sam's twenty-five reached Edmonton, crime was "disorganized" to say the least, committed mostly by people of no fixed abode against one-storey businesses on Jasper Avenue and connecting streets. The loot was limited to what could be carried away on foot. Police could be on foot too. Sam Donaghey's first beat was the inner city at night. In the morning, when newsmen met with the chief to read patrolmen's reports of the night's actions, Sam's had a uniquely Irish flavour. "When I saw Nick Gordychuk running, I thought I would run too. I called for him to stop but he redoubled the efforts of his feet." In addition to the crimes, Sam would report conversations—neat character sketches—of people he met on his rounds. These reports showed sympathy, and more than that, understanding, particularly of First Nations people.

It was this concern that brought Sam to the cause of Alec DeCoteau, the Métis runner and one-time city policeman who died in the First World War. Edmonton had a Sports Hall of Fame, but DeCoteau was not welcome, rejected by the director because he was "just an Indian." The matter of his credentials became a battle of wills, with Sam tracking down Alec DeCoteau's records, his relatives, and memorabilia such as the prize he won for voluntarily coming in second. Second prize was a violin. He let another runner win the race so he could claim second prize as a present for his sister.

The Sports Hall of Fame dug in for years but finally capitulated in 1967. Sam's campaign was not appreciated there, but in the Cree Nation around Battleford, Saskatchewan where Alec DeCoteau grew up, he was made an honorary chief with the name Man of Vision. In time, five more bands made him chief, and the Samson Band of Hobbema conferred a name with sly recognition of his paralyzing handshake—Chief Ironhand.

Ironically (my apologies for the play on words), Sam's official title for many years was police cartographer. The huge hands with the bone-crunching grip could maneuver a fine drafting pen to create intricate maps of streets and lanes in crime zones with specific details marked to assist investigations. He also organized police archives and a museum. In the community, he was Edmonton's most visible Irishman, literally and figuratively, waving the starter's pistol at a track meet, or marshalling a pack of young Irish dancers.

Wherever Sam went, he was on stage, telling stories from his vast collection. His leprechaun voice was often on radio. On St. Patrick's Day, he would come to CJCA to tape an episode of *The Edmonton Story*. I would convert Sam's tales into a script in which he would explain things Irish to a bewildered Scot, played by the city solicitor, Alan Macdonald. Sam had many stories about the south side police station, now a public health centre across from the Bus Barns market. In later years, the TV comedy series *Barney Miller* would remind him of the old south station on Saturday nights. In 1960, we had Sam recall an Irish occasion in that storied place to clarify for the Scotsman a seeming Irish contradiction: the friendly fight.

SAM Top o' the mornin', Alan.

ALAN Begorra! A genuine Irish accent on St. Patrick's Day. 'Tis a miracle. On the other hand, perhaps 'tis Constable Sam Donaghey.

SAM City of Edmonton, province of Alberta...sworn to pinch MacDonalds without fear and O'Donnell's without favour.

ALAN So top o' the morning to you, too, Sam. Though as a Scot I find more beauty in a braw bricht meenlicht nicht. In spite of that, it does seem that Irish eyes are smiling.

SAM They're a darlin' race and that's a fact.

ALAN But there's something that puzzles me about this darlin' race, Sam. At this season of the year when we are subjected to a bombardment of hearsay about Ireland, and about the darlin' race, it puzzles me that on the one hand the Irish enjoy a reputation for good nature and on the other hand enjoy an equal reputation for belligerence. As a Scot, and therefore totally logical, I find it difficult to reconcile these conflicting claims of good nature and belligerence.

SAM Oh, 'tis the glory of the race. 'Tis none but the Irish can enjoy a friendly fight.

ALAN Hmmmm. As a lawyer, as well as a Scot, "friendly fight" seems a contradiction in terms. Can you explain it?

SAM Well, I don't know as I could explain it, for that's the glory of it, like many things Irish. But I could give an example of how this beautiful thing works.

ALAN I'd appreciate that. I presume this incident occurred in Ireland.

SAM Oh no, right here, city of Edmonton, province of Alberta. It was one night about six years ago. Oh what a terrible night. Rain and wind and cold. De Valera would not 'a put Cromwell out on a night like that. I was in the south side station congratulatin' myself for bein' so shrewd as to be inside, and chattin' with Inspector Peterson.

ALAN I know Jim Peterson. A very kindly fellow. Jim and his wife run the Home for Ex-Servicemen's Children.

SAM Too true, Alan. He was known as "The Cop Who Couldn't Shoot Straight."

ALAN I was not aware of this interesting distinction. May I inquire how it was acquired?

SAM Well, it was early in his service...so early he was in North Edmonton patrollin' the stockyards at night. One time he surprised a couple o' young fellahs in the act o' breakin' into a store. They didn't stop to visit...took off on their feet with Peterson yellin' fer them to halt. They didn't, so he fired a warnin' shot. But they redoubled the efforts o' their feet. So he fired another and one o' them drops to the ground. There's pressure from city hall so Peterson is in court on the charge o' woundin' with intent.

ALAN And how did that go?

SAM Oh, it went fine. His lawyer brought in the Inspector's scores on the rifle range, which showed that he couldn't hit anything. If he'd intended to hit the fugitive, he would'a missed.

ALAN A fascinating digression, Sam, but a digression nonetheless.

SAM About the friendly fight. Well, as I said, we're in the station on this dark and stormy night, congratulatin' ourselves on bein' inside in contrast to bein' out, when the phone rings. The Inspector puts it down and he says: "Sorry, boys, ye've got to get the O'Grogans. They're disturbin' the peace o' all the neighbourhood." So we get the wagon...

ALAN The Paddy wagon, I presume.

SAM Too true, and away we go, and there they are out in the front yard, stripped to the waist and goin' at it...the five O'Grogan boys, and fine figures of Irish lads they are, rollin' in the mud and payin' no heed to the rain at all at all.

ALAN Was a little bit of heaven falling from out the sky?

SAM I shouldn't be surprised. There was everything else, and a man could scarce stand up in the road which was mud as well. The O'Grogans is flyin' this way and that. They're mud from head to toe and anything black that goes whizzin' past is an O'Grogan. So we make a bucket brigade fer to get the O'Grogans into the wagon. Lockhart is by the door, I'm next, then Davis, then Mahaffey, and Pacholak. Our strategy is to grab somethin' black which is goin' past at high speed and cussin'—and pass him man to man into the wagon. But a man that's all mud is like catchin' a greased pig. And before long ye can't tell Mahaffey and Pacholak from the O'Grogans except fer the cussin'.

ALAN   I regret sincerely that I was not a witness to this thrilling spectacle, Sam. Did you prevail?

SAM   I wouldn't exactly say we prevailed, though we did get all five into the wagon and into the cells.

ALAN   And was that the end of this Irish occasion?

SAM   Oh no. The door opens, and into the station comes none other than Mother O'Grogan.

ALAN   I can see it now, Sam. One of those sweet old Irish mithers whose sons are tenors.

SAM   Too true, Alan. And in her sweet old Irish way, she picks up a glob o' mud and wings the Inspector right betwixt the eyes.

ALAN   Just what Mother Machree would have done.

SAM   Just exact. And in her sweet old Irish way, Mother O'Grogan stands there bellerin' at the top of her lungs: "Ye dirty so-and-sos! Ye dirty so-and-sos! Ye'd no right t'interfere! Ye'd no right t'interfere! Fer they was havin' just a friendly fight!"

22

THE
CURÉ
OF
Partoutville

THE SOFT MISTY NOVEMBER AFTERNOON in 1953 wove an ideal atmosphere for going to meet the last of the old-time missionaries, the last link with Bishop Vital Grandin and the Oblate churchmen of the nineteenth century. Father Joseph Aldric Normandeau had amassed a unique title— Curé de Partoutville—pastor of Here-There-and-Everywhereville. Though he may not have been everywhere, he was certainly here and there—curé at Villeneuve, Pickardville, Legal, Vimy, Westlock, Edmonton, Beaumont, and Joussard. And he'd have been more places if he hadn't spent ten years bringing trainloads of homesteaders from Quebec to northern Alberta.

I was to meet him at St. Joseph's Hospital, a hospice for the elderly at Whyte Avenue and 107 Street, now converted to the Garneau Lofts. His window on the top floor looked north, towards hundreds of square miles where he had made history.

I was greeted by a courtly gentleman on whom seventy-nine years lay lightly, with a smile which began deep in his eyes and spread outwards. When we found chairs among the piles of paper—histories of towns and parishes and families—in the north window, the smile became confidential. "May I ask if you might be a gran'son of my friend Mr. J. J. Cashman who was at the penitentiary. You are? (The smile became a chuckle.) Ah, I mus' tell you how he fooled the warden."

In case the reader is wondering, Gramp was not an inmate of the federal penitentiary, which occupied a huge slice of real estate just east of downtown, from Jasper Avenue up to 111 Avenue. Gramp was the business manager. He and Father Normandeau became friends in 1916–1917, when the father was prison chaplain and curé of Immaculate Conception Church on 96 Street while building a new church at Beaumont. The prison conducted a lot of business. The site of Clarke Park and Commonwealth Stadium was a farm. Below ground, inmates dug coal in what was cleverly named the Penn Mine. When the warden was away, the duties of the business manager included checking his mail for anything that required immediate action. One day there came a directive from Ottawa which, in Gramp's view, required action before the warden came back. Father Normandeau chuckled at the phone call. Gramp asked: "Do you want an organ and an altar and pews for your new church? Well, have a dray here at nine o'clock tomorrow morning." Ottawa had directed the warden to donate the old chapel fittings to an appropriate church. Though the warden was a fine fellow, he was a member of the Loyal Orange Lodge. A church which acknowledged the pope would not benefit unless there was a dray on hand at nine the next morning. When the warden returned, the chapel fittings were in Beaumont. He could hardly go out and haul them back. The kind old missionary felt obvious sympathy for the warden, but when the Lord provides, what can you do?

Father Normandeau was our last personal contact with Bishop Vital Grandin and the missionary age he symbolized. The father's amusement with the warden carried over into memories of that chronic invalid, the French aristocrat whose own sense of humour helped him survive the rigours of the frontier and his draining physical afflictions.

When Father Normandeau arrived in 1902, Bishop Grandin was in his last illness, though it could be said that his last illness had begun when he was a youth in the French provincial town of Aron. At age twenty-eight, when he might reasonably have been expected to be in an early grave, Grandin was in Canada, being consecrated bishop of the territory from Manitoba to the Rockies and the Arctic. The sickly bishop would spend forty-five years travelling—by foot, canoe, dog team, snowshoe, horseback, steamboat, and buckboard wagon.

Father Normandeau arrived as transport modes of the fur trade were giving way to the mode of settlement and agriculture. His ministry of travel would be on the railways. Homesteaders were moving into northern Alberta. Bishop Grandin's successor, Emile Legal, was keen to preserve a Francophone presence. Proprietors of the railways were keen for any presence and embraced the Legal proposition that Father Normandeau organize trainloads of homestead families in his native Quebec and bring them to the land of promise at excursion rates.

When Father Normandeau wasn't building churches, he was working on the railroad, bringing in congregations. Excursions occurred in the season when the country most resembled the "Golden Granary" pictured in company brochures and the federal government's official pitch to homesteaders: the *Last Best West* magazine. (No point in showing scenes of lone farmhouses in the other season.) In that season, Father Normandeau was on the move through rural Quebec, talking up the prospects for large families squeezed onto small farms. They were invited to come and see for themselves, with no obligation to buy; if they wanted to go home, they could do so at the same cheap fare. Half a dozen times a season, a special train would leave from Montreal, a slow train, with five days for the curé to handle question after question after question—about prospects *here*, which friends had settled *there*, and what it was like *somewhere else*. By the time the First World War had cooled Alberta's first boom, he had spent four years boosting the Francophone presence. The lull offered the relaxation of being a parish priest in Edmonton, prison chaplain, and builder of a church in Beaumont.

The war ended, though not the income tax instituted to pay for it, and Father Normandeau was back on the trains. But now the journey had an extra day. Alberta was moving north, pushing two railroads into the Catholic diocese of Athabasca-Mackenzie, which extended all the way to the Arctic. The Alberta-and-Great-Waterways railroad ran to Fort McMurray. The Edmonton-Dunvegan-and-British Columbia railroad opened the Peace River Country to large-scale settlement. The northern bishop, Emile Grouard, thought a significant Francophone presence would be an asset and invited the expert to resume his ministry of the rails.

With an occasional break, Father Normandeau spent six seasons bringing trainloads and sending hundreds of "har-vest-ers" on the harvest specials, who stayed. By 1929, the father had brought and sent so many that Bishop Grouard decided he should settle in with them. The venerable bishop was ninety-three. He had been sixty-seven years in the north of the fur trade and thought a younger man should have the honour of organizing parishes, setting up credit unions, and helping the newcomers bridge the difference between farming in Quebec and on the "grande prairie." So, Joussard became the final stop for the Curé de Partoutville.

The curé's talents produced another service sought out by government and industry. It involved translation. A set of official regulations, no matter how finely crafted in one language, can give rise to derision and hilarity when poorly transferred to another. A well-knit phrase can unravel in translation. A snappy slogan or marketing name can lose its snap—which brought a farm implement company to the rectory at Joussard seeking a snapper for a new machine designed to compact the soil and prevent erosion. The name *Landpacker* had a snap to it, but all attempts to convert Landpacker to a snappy French equivalent were coming out flat and soggy. It was a problem even for the curé. But in a few months, Joussard and other Francophone communities across Canada saw the *rouleau tasseur*.

When Father Normandeau was done making history, he didn't leave it behind. His apartment above Whyte Avenue with the northward window was crammed with it. Paper, paper everywhere—in file cabinets, boxes, folders, or loose on any free surface. The history of churches, parishes, communities, families, and individuals. He explained a blank sheet on his desk with a name at the top. "When I go out," he smiled, "someone will get me to one side and say: 'Father, when I am gone you write a little piece about me. I will not be here to read it, but others will.'" So on this day, he was writing a little piece for *La Survivance*, the Francophone newspaper, and CHFA, the radio station. It was obvious there wasn't much to put in this piece, but he would do his best. It was not a burden. "When we are old," he smiled, "we have no longer ambition but only to be useful and if possible to help in the causes in which we have served."

At the handshake which ended the interview, the smile broke into a laugh. The man with so much to remember was remembering something. Was it being on a wagon in a prison yard while an organ was hoisted aboard?

23

A
Personal Family
POSTSCRIPT

FATHER NORMANDEAU'S FRIEND, Gramp Cashman, lived in a house on 124 Street, 10243–124 Street, to be precise. People used to wonder about this house, set at the very back of a 25-foot lot, in a thick grove of poplar and birch trees, a gracious habitat for squirrels and birds not too proud to accept handouts from humans. Through the centre of this mini-forest a wooden walk ran 100 feet to the front door. At age three I discovered that this walk gave off a very satisfactory thunder when run on, out to the sidewalk and back, over and over. Till the house came down for an apartment block in 1958, people wondered how it got there. I got the story from one of the chaps who put it there: Dr. Jimmy Carmichael, the whimsical dentist. Jimmy's better half was an Edmonton icon, Beatrice Van Loo, who came here in 1920 with her all-girl band to play eight weeks at the Macdonald Hotel; she stayed on to marry Jimmy and found the Edmonton Civic Opera Society.

Jimmy had arrived early in 1913 and took up batching with a couple of new lawyer friends, Sam Short and Gordon Fraser. All three were planning to make one fortune from their profession and another from the real estate boom which was raging. They rented René Lemarchand's house while he was off on a business holiday in his native Paris. When the dapper entrepreneur returned, they solved their personal housing shortage in the tight market by having a small house built—on skids. They would skid their invention to some lot they had for sale, and when it was sold, would skid to another location. They had a lot at 10243–124 Street, which they thought was worth $12,000. They were prepared to live in the woods there till they got their price.

Gramp Cashman with a visitor at the house in the trees.

The summer of 1913 was idyllic and fall was nice, but with winter approaching and no buyer in sight, they decided their house would need heat. So, they declared a basement-digging day among their friends. Two cases of Scotch whiskey attracted thirty friends, and on Thanksgiving Day, while the Edmonton Eskimos were thrashing the Calgary Tigers 13 to 12 at Diamond Park, they dug. The result was not so much a basement as a pit in which to put a furnace. The house was skidded over top and with coal, or wood from the property, the furnace kept out the cold. But when spring came in 1914, it was obvious that more than the house was on skids—so was the boom. The three bachelors walked away from their investment and let the city take the lot (and house) for unpaid taxes—along with 70,000 other lots.

It seems likely that Gramp acquired the property and contents in a tax sale. Additions were made to the bachelors' pad, including a very-low-rise foundation, a veranda with railings to which squirrels came to accept hand-outs, and the wooden walk in front, one hundred feet of it, which yielded such satisfactory thunder.

24

THE
DENTIST'S
Tale

IN AUGUST 1959, I was fortunate to obtain an appointment with Dr. "Sandy" Goodwin, the dentist. Not because I was suffering from a tooth-ache. I would be able to hear Edmonton's first dentist tell about arriving in 1891 on the second train from Calgary, what he found in Edmonton, and what he thought of the sixty-eight years which followed.

Alexander Hooper Goodwin was born at Baie Verte on New Brunswick's North Shore in 1868. Life was never easy there. From the family farm, he could look over into Nova Scotia where the people insisted proudly that life was even tougher there. Adventurous youths are attracted to new things. Young Sandy was intrigued by scientific dentistry, so new that the nearest school was six hundred miles down the coast in Baltimore. At eighteen, he set out for the University of Maryland and emerged four years later to take up the life of a travelling dentist, touring the North Shore in a democrat, seeking teeth in need of his skills.

A few months of travel persuaded him that he should find a place to settle and let patients come to *him*. An older brother knew the Taylors, S.S. and H.C., lawyers who had gone to the Northwest Territories to practice law in Edmonton. Sandy wrote the Taylor brothers. They wrote back assuring him that Edmonton was a go-ahead place with a future and a long list of needs—including a dentist. That's how, on August 31, 1891, he found himself aboard the second train from Calgary to Edmonton. A fellow passenger, also twenty-three, was G. R. F. Kirkpatrick, Edmonton's first bank manager.

The journey was eighteen hours of fascination. The train stopped often, anywhere, sometimes nowhere, so that a homesteading family could get off, have their livestock and farm equipment unloaded, and strike off towards their piece of the promised land. Sandy began the long day riding in the caboose, the equivalent of first class, but was soon on the roof of the nearest boxcar, watching the empty plains, then the empty forests, roll away on either side. For the young man from New Brunswick's North Shore, there was something of the sea about it. He felt curiously at home.

Getting down to business at his destination, he opened Edmonton's first dental clinic at 97 Street and Jasper Avenue, renting the front parlour of a log house owned by Mrs. Kelly. The house was literally on Jasper Avenue and had to be towed away eventually when the avenue was straightened. The rent was ten dollars a month, but Mrs. Kelly often had to wait for it. Sandy pulled teeth for fifty cents apiece and got paid half the time—if he waited long enough.

Plates, the old name for dentures, were fifteen dollars. Because fees for pulling the original teeth were deducted from the price of the plate, he seldom made a profit there. One winter, a trader in the Peace River Country sent a broken plate to be repaired. Dr. Goodwin vulcanized it into one piece again. On the return trip, the messenger sat on it and cracked it to bits. The trader decided teeth weren't worth the effort and didn't bother to replace them.

Dentistry was not painless. The only anesthetic available was sold next door in the bar of the Jasper House, where most gentlemen patients got themselves anesthetized before their appointments. Dr. Goodwin tried the new laughing gas. He bought a tank of it from a firm in Toronto but threw it out after a few experiments left the patients in worse shape than they would have been without it. Laughing gas made the patient almost hysterically elated by pumping an extra load of oxygen into the system. When a young girl went berserk, Dr. Goodwin decided that laughing gas was no laughing matter and took the rest of it to the dump. There was little wonder that people were slow about going to the dentist, so slow that Dr. Goodwin had to revert to travelling at times, riding the train as far south as Lacombe. When business was dull, he would put in the time chasing fires with the Volunteer Fire Brigade...or playing cards with the boys in the room above Emmanuel Raymer's jewellery store.

Dr. Goodwin's only competition came from a travelling charlatan— the Amazing, the Incredible Dr. True—who used to hit town about twice a year with two ladies and a drum and a set of tongs. The Incredible Dr. True was late-thirtyish with a Buffalo Bill haircut, pale face, piercing eyes, and even more piercing voice. He would ride up and down Jasper Avenue beating the drum till he drew a crowd. Then he'd exhibit a basket of bills. For five dollars, you could stick your hand in and have a chance of pulling out a twenty. Then he'd sell charms—to ward off every affliction, including pain. If you bought a charm, the Amazing Dr. True would yank one of your teeth—right there on the spot—to prove that the charm warded off pain. People who bought the charms didn't want to admit they'd been taken in, so they'd testify that the extraction hadn't hurt a bit. He used the same tongs for every tooth and between operations would clean them on his trousers. Dr. Goodwin got some business out of the Amazing Dr. True's dentistry—treating infections and fishing out broken roots.

Dr. True made his last appearance in Edmonton in 1896. He was giving his sales talk at First Street and Jasper Avenue one fine evening, when a rugged individual named Matheson began to heckle. The Incredible Dr. True should have ignored Matheson, but as the heckler got personal, so did he. Before you could say: "Open wide! Now close!" they were rolling in the dust, in a ding-dong boxing-rassling match that collected a bigger crowd than any of Dr. True's previous shows. He emerged the clear loser and never came back, leaving Sandy Goodwin alone in the field of dentistry.

But the patients continued to leave him alone too. By 1900, the population had grown to perhaps three thousand at best, and fortune was eluding Edmonton's first dentist. So he went farming near Vegreville. He caught real estate fever for a while. When that cooled down, he came back to dentistry in 1913.

Edmonton has nineteen hundred dentists now. But Alexander Hooper Goodwin will always be Number One.

25

THE
First
CIRCUS

IN THE LATE AUGUST days before the first circus came to town, advance men were working the backroads decorating barns and fences, and anything abandoned, with startling posters. A black monster emerged from a tropic lagoon with a terrified native in its cruel jaws, while other terrified natives ran for their lives. In areas where English was not understood, a postmaster might translate the message in the bold black letters:

> The Bovalupus, rarest, strangest, awfulest of all mighty monsters of the great deep.
> Surely coming and will exhibit at South Edmonton on Saturday August 27.

The posters shouted other wonders of Lemen Brothers Circus, but the most talked-about attraction was, well, just talked about, in a confidential manner. This attraction had been the cause of an uproar at the Chicago World's Fair, and—wink-wink, nudge-nudge—the Lemen Brothers wouldn't want to have trouble in Edmonton. Didn't a wise man once say that word-of-mouth was the best advertising?

Ara Elsey arrived in Edmonton four days ahead of the circus, amid the buzz of anticipation. On the fifty-seventh anniversary of the monster show, in his farm home at Waskatenau, he told me of his first impressions of Edmonton, what he saw and what he heard.

People were talking about the circus and the Klondike Gold Rush, which was in high gear in August 1898. Farmers he met wanted to tell him about the record oats crop, a bumper crop that grew out of despair. The oats seemed doomed by a hot, dry summer. Roots were turning brown. No rain fell till June 23. It was a little rain, but every day for the next two months a little rain fell from cool, cloudy skies. As a result, the best oats crop ever was standing in the fields, ripe for harvest. Ara heard the story so often, it seemed that all farmers must have suspended the harvest to see the terrible Bovalupus and other wonders the Lemen Brothers had brought. Circuses travelled on railways. The Calgary and Edmonton Railway ended in Old Stratchcona, so the "waterproof" tents were pitched on a field southwest of the station.

The Bovalupus was, to put it gently, oversold. It was in a tank and seemed to be asleep. While it wasn't exactly handsome, it was hardly big enough to be the rarest, strangest, awfulest monster of the mighty deep. Indians were contemptuous. Most viewers took it as a joke. The word Bovalupus was obviously concocted by the Lemen Brothers. If it meant anything, it was Cow-Wolf. But hurry-hurry-hurry, other attractions were calling. Shows in the big tent were at ten in the morning and six in the evening. Rajah the Elephant was perhaps not the biggest brute on earth, mightier than the famous Jumbo, but quite satisfactory. Perhaps Captain Santiago didn't make his famous backward dive from the highest height ever, but it was high enough. And there was no sham about Little Edna the Wonder Girl doing somersaults on the back of a galloping horse, or Kitty Kruger driving six horses at once. The show was well worth a dollar with fifty cents extra for a reserved seat—in an age when a quart of Scotch whiskey was a dollar.

That was the show under "the big top." Under a smaller top occurred the phenomenon too explosive to advertise in print. The barker lured the curious with the facts that those who entered the tent would be thrilled by the national dance of Turkey...and it would be performed by a young lady direct from that mysterious country. (Chicago must have been in Turkey then.) Those curious enough to pay became witness to gyrations which sent tremors rolling through the World's Fair. On August 27, 1898, frontier Edmonton experienced the hootchi-kootchi.

26

Bylaw
1094

TOWARDS MARCH 19 EACH YEAR, the return of the swallows to Capistrano is awaited with eager anticipation. It's a big show; scenes are televised world-wide. Each year, it brings to mind that Edmonton once had a bird show with a large cast that was awaited with eager anticipation...by the birds. But not by city officials. They might not have minded so much if the birds had come once a year, but they came once a day, to the Market Square. At ten-thirty every morning, officials could watch from the windows of city hall (on the site of the Winspear Centre) as birds congregated on the block now occupied by the Stanley A. Milner Library.

If the birds had been exotic, or cute, feelings might have been different. But they were pigeons, and there are certain disadvantages to pigeons.

The show began in a small way one day in the 1930s when Mrs. Mary Sather scattered a few crumbs for a few birds. The next day, there were a few more...and a few more...and quite a few more...and a lot more...and a heckuva lot more till it seemed that every pigeon in Edmonton had discovered the welfare state.

Birds with good homes to go to were there; pigeons who scratched a living around grain elevators arrived in whirring formations. A group of three elevators dominated the south side skyline. (The Ritchie Mill still stands, protected by an historic designation.) As ten-thirty approached each day, there was a stir which became a rustle which became a whir as the resident pigeons rose up from the elevators and streaked for the Market Square. Streaked is appropriate. A pigeon waddling on the ground doesn't look athletic but in the air can hit fifty to seventy kilometres per hour and outrace a hungry peregrine falcon.

Let's join the pigeons for a bird's eye view of the landing. With two blocks to go, the chateau roof of the Macdonald Hotel is below. In the block ahead, the McLeod Building is coming up on the left. Directly below is the Post Office, with the clock tower that will one day mark the entrance to the Westin Hotel. Then the Market Square is below, a city block framed on all four sides by wooden buildings, mostly one storey with no basement, housing forty-five small businesses. On the west side of the square is the Market building, a long, low, brick shed with doors that close with a bang. On the east side are the farm wagons with their horses, and Mrs. Mary Sather with her bag of the good things in life.

The birds dined well in all seasons but best in winter, when the menu was wheat. Each morning, Mrs. Sather would call in at the Capital Seed store (where the Lee Pavilion of the Citadel Theatre is), and buy a sack of wheat, fifty pounds. On days of extreme winter, she would ask the seed men to handle the distribution. They were glad to oblige such a good customer.

But city hall was watching and hearing from spoilsports who dwelt on the disadvantages of pigeons. The city solicitor was asked to draft a bylaw which would anticipate and close every legal loophole through which Mary Sather could slip snacks to her friends. On January 14, 1946, Bylaw 1094 came to city council. From then on, it was illegal to *put*, *place*, *scatter*, or *distribute* pigeon food in the Market. The city remained wary of pigeons coming back. Bylaw 1094 stayed on the books until 1985, twenty years after the library took over their square.

27

THE

SCOTS

Boarding House

THE AGE OF THE BOARDING HOUSE was the age of young men outnumbering young women, from about 1905 to the early 1920s. In some, the cook-housekeeper was an employee of a band of young fellows on their way up in the business world. In others, the cook-housekeeper was a no-nonsense den mother, like Mrs. Rennie of the Scots boarding house. The specialty of this house was young teamsters fresh from Scotland. There wasn't much of Mary Rennie, but there was never a moment of doubt of who was in charge.

Mary did not arrive in Edmonton with the intention of running a Scots boarding house. That came of one of those best-laid plans which gang aft agley. Mary and her husband, Alex, were raising five boys and four girls on a small farm in Aberdeenshire. Mary's brother, Peter Cruikshank, had gone out to Edmonton in 1901. He was a teamster with a horse-drawn delivery wagon. He wrote home enthusiastic reports about Alberta and the opportunities for Mary's family.

So Alex and Mary Rennie laid a plan. He was near fifty, she near forty. He would go ahead to Edmonton to find a house; the family would join him; and when they'd adjusted to the new surroundings, they would go into the countryside and claim one of those 160-acre homesteads for ten dollars.

Alex found a house on Fraser Avenue—which became 98 Street and eventually disappeared under Canada Place, the Citadel Theatre, Winspear Centre, and the Court House. Mary liked the sound of Fraser Avenue, so reassuring to Scottish ears. Till she saw it, on April 1, 1908. Mud was so intense that the horses had to rest twice in the three blocks from Jasper Avenue. Mary was astounded when two weeks of the sunshine that Peter had written about baked the mud into ruts as dry and hard as the Stone of Scone.

The homestead plan went quickly agley. The Rennies saw it wasn't practical for a family that large, and there was also the matter of schools. The Scots ranked education with food among the necessities of life—ahead of food if necessary. The children would have to remain in Edmonton, and Mary was not about to leave the girls in a city of bachelors.

So Alex got a job. He could handle horses, and so joined Peter in driving teams for City Transfer. The brothers-in-law became specialists, delivering baggage for passengers arriving at the train stations. In those years, people tended to pack everything but the grand piano when they went visiting. Wagons were heavy with trunks, hat boxes, canvas hold-alls, and wooden crates nailed shut. Edmonton was growing, but not so much that two men couldn't handle the baggage. Alex went west; Peter went east. The cartage business was growing, along with most others. When the brothers-in-law encountered among the arriving passengers a young newcomer from Scotland, they directed him to their employer, Bert Potter. Bert was not a Scot but, as the Scots put it, he was smart enough to marry one. He appreciated the young men from the misty glens; they came lean and wiry, accustomed to hard work, long hours, and long winters.

Bert lived across the street from the Rennies in a bigger house, much bigger. Business was so good that he built himself one bigger yet and made Alex and Mary a surprising proposition. They should move into the place he was leaving and make it into a boarding house for young Scots teamsters.

As Bert expected, the lads thrived on Mary's cooking. They could rise at six, as they had at home, for breakfast like mother used to make—simple, honest oatmeal porridge salted like mackerel. There's something straightforward about oatmeal, unambiguous, free of pretense. At noon, the rigs rattled into the yard, and the lads clattered into the house for honest Scotch broth built on beef, not the mutton foisted on an unsuspecting public by the soup industry. The noon meal was dinner, coming in the middle of twelve-hour work days. At supper, when Mary Rennie offered honest oatcakes, they were eaten faster than she could put them through the oven. At Christmas, the turkey was stuffed with honest oatmeal dressing, no namby-pamby bread crumbs for the Scots boarding house.

Days began before six in the morning and ended past midnight, when the last train had been met, baggage delivered, and the last team was in the stables. The stables were on the lane behind the house. Alex Rennie was in charge there.

Despite the long hours of work, there was entertainment at the house, mostly homemade and mostly of a particular ethnic character. Arthur Miller was a boarder with talent, not the playwright but the real Arthur Miller, the piper who was to herald the coming of so many haggises on Burns Nights of the future. And there was a piano around which the boys would gather to sing. Mary Rennie enjoyed the heartbreaking songs of the homeland, but there was a downside. The lads would get homesick and go out and get drunk.

The only Irishman to dwell in this enclave provided some entertainment. Jimmy Warmington was a small man with black wavy hair and the gift of blarney. He was a streetcar conductor—proud as all creation of his blue uniform, it was said. On cold days when the streetcars couldn't run, he would be in the house teasing Mary and the daughters. On one cold day, the girls were practising with a camera. They put one of their coats on Jimmy plus a flowered hat. He was so amused by the picture that he sent it to his best girl in Ireland and wrote on it, "My best girl in Edmonton." Some jokes fall flat. This joke ballooned to a transatlantic storm. His Irish colleen didn't recognize him, with predictable results. When the tumult and the shouting died, she took no chances. She came for the wedding, and Mary lost her only Irish boarder.

In Henderson's 1910 Directory, 342 Fraser Avenue appears as *bdg hse*, but it was more than that, often an infirmary. Mary nursed sore throats, sore backs, cuts, bruises, and disorders of the stomach. Hospitals were not free, and Workmen's Compensation did not come into the picture till 1918. One day, a lad named Johnny Sutherland was brought in on a stretcher. He had fallen in a dark stairway moving a heavy trunk. The trunk splintered his shoulder. The doctor who came said: "Can you take care of him here? He is your son." "No," she said, "he is a boarder. But when something like this happens, they are all my sons."

There was, however, a memorable occasion when she lost patience with them, the whole bunch simultaneously. Sharp at eleven o'clock on the morning of May 26, 1919, all the whistles in town started blowing. She wondered what the noise was about but had little time to wonder; she was busy preparing the hearty dinner the lads would need to continue their work. They came clattering in, excited about the whistling. It was a signal to begin a general strike in sympathy with comrades involved in the general strike at Winnipeg. Everybody was out in sympathy except the police, firemen, and printers. Even the bootleggers were out.

The strikers got no sympathy from their landlady. In a burst of fury, she told them that if they were on strike, then she was on strike too. They couldn't expect any more food until they went back to work. And they couldn't expect to lie around the boarding house, idling away the hours. They could come home only to sleep. Mary Rennie meant every angry word, but she was up against another of those plans which gang swift agley. Retelling the story forty years after, she said: "I had them scared...for once. But I couldn't hold out. I loved them all."

THE
LAWYER'S
Tale

THE IDEA OF JUSTICE is presented by a classic icon—a young woman, eyes cloaked in a blindfold, displays the scales. It's a symbol recognized through the ages and throughout the world. But in the 1890s, another symbol of justice was recognized in Edmonton—a tin bathtub roped to the carriage which brought passengers from the railway to the Alberta Hotel. If a hotel guest wanted a bath, he brought his own tub. This tub gave public notice that Judge David Lynch Scott was arriving to conduct a session of the High Court of the Northwest Territories.

Fred Jamieson was there to watch the judicial bathtub arrive. Fred was there to observe and participate in all processes of the law. Happily for us, he was *here*…sixty years after…to give eyewitness accounts of events and personalities of that delightful time. On the frosted glass of his office door in the McLeod Building, he was F.C. Jamieson QC. To old friends, he was Freddie. To the city at large, he was Colonel Jamieson, from his long service as a citizen-soldier, beginning with the cavalry in the Boer War. His figure was short but conveyed quiet power. He was quiet in speech too, and his pace was unhurried, matching nicely the rhythms of judicial process that he observed in the 1890s.

When Fred left Ontario in 1893, he came to Lacombe, proposing to be a farmer. Three years on a homestead, however, convinced him the west must have something better to offer, and he wrote hopefully to an old neighbour from Carleton County. A.C. Rutherford was practising law on Whyte Avenue. Mr. Rutherford, who would be first premier of Alberta, had a law

Fred Jamieson as a younger man.

Provincial Archives of Alberta Info file, Jamieson, Frederick Charles

degree from McGill, whereas the first prime minister of Canada, Sir John A. Macdonald, had "read for the law" in the office of a cousin.

Rutherford offered Fred an opportunity to "take the low road," like John A. had. At a salary of five dollars a week—which went far enough—Fred would handle office paperwork and read law books till he'd absorbed enough to try the bar examinations. Most lawyers had a typewriter but young lady stenographers were not yet available, so Fred mastered a modern technology to type letters, wills, codicils, caveats, land transfers, and statutory declarations.

There was no hurry for these instruments, or anything else, in the office or outside on Whyte Avenue. Fred had plenty of hours to read for the law. If he shut the office for an hour and went to the Strathcona Hotel for a beer, no one noticed. When court was sitting, he attended sessions, and there was no hurry in that sector either.

The court shared space with almost every social and entertainment activity in Edmonton. Robertson's Hall and Opera House was above a wholesale on Jasper Avenue at 97 Street, across from the present Hardware Grill. On a Wednesday, for example, this versatile facility could be a courtroom by day, and at night a dance hall jumping to the tunes of Jack the Whistler, virtuoso of the tin whistle. On a Thursday, it could be a courtroom by day and a scene of a patent medicine show at night. After court on Friday, there could be a lecture hall for Pauline Johnson, the Métis poet.

Second-storey justice was unhurried. Court reporters were not yet part of the process. Judges wrote down testimony in longhand. "Wait a minute, wait a minute," Judge Scott would intone. "Wait a minute. Very well, proceed, Mr. Beck." Local business moved at about the same pace. Scott Robertson, who owned Robertson's Hall, engaged in insurance and other enterprises, but the low pressure of business allowed time for his official duties as sheriff of the judicial district, and he attended all sessions. Court records were kept in a filing cabinet in the office of Alex Taylor. His duties as postmaster and owner of the town's telephone and electric light companies allowed all the time needed for official duties as clerk of the court. He would take down examinations-for-discovery in longhand.

The hall setting encouraged relaxation of the formality expected in courthouses with stone pillars in front. Judge Scott was fond of what in the plays of Shakespeare are called "asides." One day, he presided at the trial of a young man who'd drawn a knife during a fight. The opponent was not stabbed seriously but enough to convict his assailant. Judge Scott said: "Eighteen months." The accused said: "____ ____ ____ ____!" In an aside to the entire assembly, including Fred Jamieson, the judge said: "He's appealing to a higher court."

Among our handful of lawyers was one who didn't find any of this amusing. Charles Lewis Shaw was better known as an author who wrote most feelingly about the petty drudgery of law practice on the frontier. Captain O'Brien, however, thought it was just fine. O'Brien was the lone Irishman in a party of English aristocrats who arrived in 1897 en route to the Klondike Gold Rush. He was invited to leave the party when he threatened the leader with an axe. The Mounted Police magistrate then invited him to get out of Edmonton within twenty-four hours. Captain O'Brien complied by taking the ferry across the river and hanging his shingle on Whyte Avenue, down the street from A.C. Rutherford.

The captain had the advantage of special knowledge when he began his practice. Fred Jamieson saw how valuable it was watching justice snail past in Robertson's Hall. Knowledge of law was not enough for a successful lawyer. He must know almost as much about horses. All human activity, commerce, agriculture, transportation—depended on the horse. Disputes about horses put a constant strain on the legal and judicial systems. A lawyer had to know everything about brands and branding. He had to know every possible colour a hide could take and the word for each in English, French, German, Polish, and Mexican. He had to know as much as a veterinarian about the diseases to which horse flesh is subject. In every issue of the *Bulletin* were notices about lost, stolen, and strayed horses. The Edmonton district had a particular problem with strays. Most farm animals were trailed up from Montana or southern Alberta. On getting loose, a Montana horse would head for its old home on the range.

Allegations of horse-trader misconduct took Fred to Red Deer for a memorable occasion. While Robertson's Hall was no palace, the arrangement in Red Deer made it seem so. A courtroom had been contrived by partitioning part of a hotel bar. The judicial bathtub was in an upstairs room. Judge Scott was there to hear the case. But sounds of revelry from the other side of the partition mounted so high that he couldn't hear much of anything, including testimony of witnesses. So he had to adjourn the case till next morning—early next morning, because the bar opened at six.

Other animals could be the stuff of court proceedings too. On June 12, 1899, the *Bulletin* reported the trial of an alleged pig rustler…in which the pig gave evidence for the prosecution. Here, word for word, is the story which delighted Fred Jamieson and everyone who read or heard about it:

A rather novel case was heard by N. McIntyre, J.P. on Monday last at the police barracks, in which the ownership of a pig of very tender age was the subject of a dispute. The pig and his mother were the chief witnesses in the case, and although their evidence was not under oath it was considered the best produced by either party, and on its strength a certain young man in town was fined five dollars and costs. The little pig, when put in the pen of hogs from which it was charged he had been taken, hunted out his mother, and his place by her side, with an instinct quite interesting to behold, and which contradicted in a most convincing manner the story of the accused.

That was June 1899. In August, Frederick C. Jamieson was admitted to the bar of the Northwest Territories. He became a partner of his mentor, A.C. Rutherford, and won his first case…without saying a word. He had climbed the stairs to Robertson's Hall to defend a slight sixteen-year-old boy charged with forcing his attentions on a lady twice his size. Justice Rouleau listened to the prosecutor's story. Fred was rising to launch his well-prepared defense when the justice held up his hand for silence. He looked from the slight defendant to the fiercely buxom accuser, and back to the accused. He shook his head and smiled. "Dis is ri-*dicka*-lose. Da case is dismiss."

29

Presgrave Winter's
TALE

YOU MIGHT CALL Presgrave Winter an executive cowboy. As the nineteenth century rolled into the twentieth, he used to put on rodeos on Jasper Avenue.

At birth, he would seem the lad least likely to become a cowboy. He was born in Cheltenham, England, in 1870, the sixth son of the Reverend Christopher Winter. Presgrave would seem destined for a quiet life not far from his beginnings, but by 1882 there were five more young Winters for a total of eleven. Their father decided the family had better move to Canada... where there was more room.

This decision brought them to western Manitoba, to a farm near Birtle. The boys had to learn many new things, including the art of controlling oxen. On the frontier their carefully-instilled politeness never deserted them. If Percy, the eldest, shouted "Gee!" and the ox went the other way, Percy would say: "Oh, I beg your pardon. I meant 'Haw!'"

The boys grew up polite, but fast. At thirteen, Presgrave was working for the local storekeeper. In trading with the Natives he became fluent speaking Cree or Sioux. At eighteen years of age, he was an interpreter for the North West Mounted Police in Regina. At twenty, he was in the ranch country of southern Alberta learning about horses. He spent a winter alone with a hundred horses, breaking them for the spring sales. He spent an educational year with "Professor" Bell, a noted eccentric, from whom he learned the *quiet-breaking* method. The conventional mode was anything but quiet. Get a rope on the critter, haul him down, drag him around to hootin' and hollerin' of participants and spectators. The "Professor's" approach was calm and reassuring. Instead of throwing the horse, he rode it. And instead of one rope, he had four—one attached to each foot. If the critter started to gallop or rear, he'd pull on one foot and the horse would have to stop or fall down.

At twenty-five, Pres Winter was in business for himself. There wasn't much he didn't know about horses, and he had a firm grasp of the economics of horse-trading. Go down to Montana, buy one hundred horses for one hundred dollars, and watch them appreciate in value as they're trailed north. By Fort Macleod, a one-dollar horse was a five-dollar horse. And at the end of the trail in Edmonton, it was a *twenty*-five dollar horse. Pres also had an instinct for marketing. At towns on the trail, he and his riders would put on a rodeo on the main street to advertise their farm horses.

Twice a year, Pres brought his rodeo to Jasper Avenue, a main thoroughfare surfaced only with the rich black loam that attracted homesteaders. The merchandise would go into a corral at 95 Street. Then it was on to the rodeo by the Queen's Hotel—across from Canada Place. The horses of Pres's riders became bucking broncos for the occasion. Spectators crowded the hotel balconies and threw silver dollars to their favourites. When the professionals had done their show, the saloon cowboys were invited to try. And when the last amateur bit the dust of Jasper Avenue, the show moved to the corral for the sales.

In his business dealings, Presgrave Winter adhered strictly to the horse-trader's code of honour: Never take advantage of an earnest, unsophisticated settler but take every possible advantage of another horse-trader because he's trying to do the same to you.

All rodeos were exciting for spectators, but one turned out to be exciting for Presgrave Winter. He was a perceptive judge of horses, but he could also recognize a spectator who was not merely enjoying the action but understanding and appreciating the qualities of the horses and the skills of their riders. His performers were raising dust on the main street of Wetaskiwin when he noted such a person in the crowd. He noted further that she was about twenty, and excitement made her even more attractive.

Pres decided that he must meet this girl. Or rather, he must seek an introduction through her family. Ever the Victorian gentleman, he would proceed by the usual channels. The introduction was an immediate success... though Pres spoke only English and Marie Mathilde Dupuis spoke only French. The universal language of love bridged the gap till he could take his bride to their home on a ranch west of Lacombe.

While marriage was changing Presgrave's lifestyle, development was changing his business style. The city of Edmonton put down pavement over his rodeo ground. On country roads of the new province, herds of travelling horses were not as welcome as they had been. But the government was promoting railways, and he brought horses in by the trainload. He was into racing with an impressive stable of thoroughbreds, and as a sideline had horse-drawn taxis in Lacombe. He was proud of the smart rigs and bragged of gold teeth possessed by two of his drivers: "Even my drivers are gold-plated."

While the world changed around him, Presgrave Winter maintained links with his Victorian upbringing, dressing for dinner on the ranch, attending country dances in white tie and tails. But with it all, he cherished a link with his days as an executive cowboy. He smoked chewing tobacco. He would chip flakes from the dark plug and catch them in the bowl of his pipe. There they would burn as a rough incense, recalling campfires on the trail and rodeos on Jasper Avenue.

30

AN
UPHILL
Battle

FROM 1920, INTO THE 1960S, Pat Patrick was caretaker of the W.W. Arcade Building. In his room above the present Hardware Grill, preparing to brew coffee for a visitor, Pat knew better than anyone in Edmonton the wonder of turning on a tap. Today and every day, EPCOR pumps 260 million litres (58 million gallons) of water into a system which is almost out of sight and, therefore, out of mind—except for the taps. But water distribution was highly visible when Pat arrived in Edmonton. Highly visible—and highly audible—in the first attempt to introduce technology to the process. Pat could tell about it from the viewpoint of superintendent, mechanical engineer, steam engineer, fireman, bookkeeper, clerk, and part owner. From his second-storey window, he could look down on Jasper Avenue at 97 Street and on down to the river, pointing out the locations of the components of the water system.

Christened Emerson Theodore Patrick, "Pat" came off a farm near London, Ontario which grew a bumper crop of young Patricks—eleven in all. Pat figured there was no room for him there but should be in the west, and after seven years en route, he reached Edmonton in 1896. He found work with an economic force in the town of perhaps 2,000. Jim Powell had a finger in more pies than you could throw in a Laurel and Hardy comedy. He had the agency for the International Harvester Company, and owned livery stables, mines, and parts of other things. If Jim had been the sort to wake up with a "Thought for Today," it would have been an idea to make money.

Pat found much to interest him in Edmonton, including the water distribution system. Water was delivered home to home by free enterprisers with tank carts. In summer Pat watched them back their carts into the river and scoop it a pail at a time into their tanks. The water was unfiltered, untreated…also unpolluted by industry or agriculture upstream. And it was free. In winter the river was scooped from cuts in the ice.

Afterwards, in all seasons, Pat witnessed a cruel demonstration of the fact that water won't run uphill. The watermen's horses, one to a cart, struggled to drag their loads up Grierson Hill (then called Cliff Street), 150 feet to the top where the customers were.

Whereas Pat saw struggling horses, Jim Powell saw another pie in which he could have a finger. If you could figure a way to make the river run uphill, just to the top, the watermen would pay to fill up there and spare themselves and their horses the ordeal of Cliff Street.

You would need a tank at the top and some sort of engine below. Pat found the engine for twenty dollars. There was a gold dredge on the river, hauling up gravel and washing it for "colour." The operation had begun with an old steam engine which had proved too small for the job. It was rusting on the bank. When Pat came along and offered twenty dollars for it, the dredgermen thought they'd put one over on the greenhorn. But he mounted it on a barge and put it to the test. If it couldn't raise gravel, it could definitely lift water.

Meanwhile, up above at 97 Street and Jasper Avenue, Jim's tank was making a visible impact on the skyline. The tank was big, enough for 50,000 gallons, and loomed larger because it was on stilts. Water runs downhill; get it overhead and gravity is your friend. In 1900 the system was complete—at both ends. All that was missing was the pipe in-between. No problem for Jim Powell. He talked town officials into "lending" him seven hundred feet of two-inch pipe, and granting him an exclusive franchise till such time as they got around to it themselves.

Pat's engine worked as well as Jim's ploy. Pat spent mornings on the river, an hour or so stoking coal to raise steam in the twenty-dollar capital investment, an hour or so listening to chawnk chawnk chawnk chawnk

chawnk chawnk chawnk as it made water run uphill. Then he spent afternoons and evenings selling it. The watermen paid a dollar for a fill-up and went on their rounds of homes, most of which had two barrels at the back door—one with rainwater for washing, the other with river water for drinking and cooking. Toilet tanks were not yet a factor.

In 1903 a plebiscite set the town system in motion. The vote was not unanimous—some crusty old-timers had little use for water externally or internally—but it carried. Pat's pumping machine on the barge gave way to a land-based plant in Rossdale, and Pat went on to other things. But the watermen remained on the job. In the city which Edmonton became in 1904, pipelayers couldn't quite keep up to house builders. Against all reasonable expectation, the city recognized the work of the watermen as an essential service. Special hydrants were provided. They came up out of the ground like inverted Letter J's. The watermen were given keys to help themselves, free. "Boots" Jones, Joe Hellman, and "Professor" Brenton carried on with the growing parade of men with horses who delivered the needs of the city—the milkman, the breadman, the iceman, the vegetable man, the junk man, the delivery man—all the big stores had one. Pat Patrick saw it happen. From his window above the Hardware Grill, he could see it all again.

31

THE
DIAMOND
King

PON YEN, THE DIAMOND KING, was unique among the founders of Edmonton. Other founders came once and stuck. Pon Yen came twice.

In 1890, when Pon Yen was seventeen, he got as far as Vancouver. Like many young men out of China, he found work in cafés and advanced to the status of cook. For three years he was cook in the home of H. H. Carry, a big man in the Canadian Pacific Railway. With the savings of eleven years of hard work, Pon returned to China to marry a girl from his village.

It's said that truth can be stranger than fiction. If proof is required, consider the fact that in the village, he met a man from Edmonton. Sam Sing was also on a home visit, with tales of his fourteen years in Edmonton. He was full of booster spirit for the town, which was a go-ahead place which couldn't miss becoming a great city. Pon must forget about Vancouver. He must come to Edmonton and be Sam Sing's partner in the Victoria Café, which was named for the capital of Hong Kong, not British Columbia.

Pon came to Edmonton alone. He was in a position to bring his bride, but as he explained gently six decades later: "She was a shy girl. She was afraid to leave her home and go to a land where people looked strange and talked funny." Then followed a patient smile which added, without words: "...the way white people think of China."

In 1902 the railway couldn't take him all the way to Edmonton. It ran only to Strathcona, where the tiny wooden station and mud of Whyte Avenue were not encouraging. But here he was glad to meet Mah Chung, the first of his countrymen to reach northern Alberta (in 1886). Across the avenue from Mah Chung's laundry, Pon met Mah Lee in his café. Then he boarded a horse-drawn bus for the bumpy ride and ferry crossing to Edmonton. The jumble of false fronts along Jasper Avenue was no more encouraging. He found Sam Sing's Victoria Café (on the site of Canada Place), across from Charlie Mah's laundry. Living in steam seven days a week Charlie washed long underwear for ten cents, cotton shirts for six cents, and shirts with starched collars for ten. Around on 101 Street was Kong Tung's café. That was the extent of the Chinese business community, and the rest of the town was in proportion. Pon Yen failed to see any evidence of the budding metropolis Sam Sing had described. In a few weeks, he was off to Nelson, home of the B.C. silver boom.

After three years of cooking for the Kootenay General Hospital, Pon saved enough for a trip to China to visit his wife. This second visit home demonstrated the axiom that history repeats itself. Against any calculable odds there was a man from Edmonton visiting the village of Mah Mee Lee. And he was saying everything Sam Sing had said three years before. Edmonton was a go-ahead place which couldn't miss becoming a great city. Pon Yen must forget about Nelson and head straight for the place with the future.

Pon had heard it all before, but the Chinese love a gamble. The second time, he found the prospect more encouraging. There was still no pavement on Jasper (or any other) Avenue, but brick buildings were going up, a transcontinental railway was approaching from the east, and the city was to be a capital.

Sam Sing's offer of partnership was still open. Edmonton "went ahead," as he'd said it would. The Victoria Café prospered. The partners built a combined café, grocery store, and Chinese social club. They had a fruit store in Camrose. They bought a grocery store in Saskatoon, and that led to a café in Prince Albert. Pon Yen had a busy sideline as an interpreter, bridging languages in hundreds of court cases, criminal and civil. He was called to Prince Albert when Chinese partners in a café had a falling out and one fatally stabbed the other. When the surviving partner was convicted of murder, the white man who owned the café asked Pon if he'd take it over. The owner's name was Diefenbaker and, yes, he had a son named John.

Business was so rewarding that Pon Yen could indulge his fascination with diamonds. He liked to collect diamonds, buy and sell them, and wear them—on rings, cufflinks, tiepins. He could afford more visits to the home village, where there was now a family. Passing through Hong Kong, he could search for stones of unusual cut—and unusual colour. He liked to tell about the canary yellow diamond, five-and-a-half carats, cut in the shape of a heart.

He bought it for twelve hundred dollars. He enjoyed having it then sold it to a man in Vancouver for six thousand dollars. That man sold it to a man in Seattle for ten thousand. And it travelled through a number of hands before reaching its final buyer in New York, who paid one hundred thousand. Listeners would try to commiserate with Pon Yen over his loss, but he told them that wasn't the point of the story. Nobody had lost. The man he bought it from made a profit; he made a profit; the man he sold it to made a profit. That was how it should be with diamonds.

The title Diamond King was awarded by the press...in the turbulent tenure of Police Chief George Hill (1914–1920). The chief was an autocratic Scot who seemed to be at war with everybody. Within three days of his arrival, he was at war with Pon Yen...over gambling. Gambling was illegal, but reasonable people recognized that Chinese men away from their families were entitled to enjoy the national pastime as long as it stayed within their clubs. The chief proved unreasonable. He gave Pon three days to "clean up Chinatown"—that is, stop the fan-tan games in the social club—or face the wrath of George Hill. He had wrath to burn; Pon's intransigence brought on seven court actions, civil and criminal, in which he was either complainant or defendant, aided by lawyers who were at war with the chief— notably Fighting Joe Clarke, the Champion of the Underdog. From every case, in whatever capacity, Pon Yen emerged triumphant. The *Bulletin* headline advised readers: Diamond King Wins Again!

Life got even better for The King. In 1918 his wife consented to join him so that their teenage son could grow up in Canada. And Pon Yen continued to add friends to his impressive list. The friendship he was most proud of came of a chance meeting in Vancouver. It was about 1925. He and

H.H. Carry passed each other on the street. It had been thirty years since Pon worked in his kitchen, but the railroad builder recognized him and greeted him as an old friend. They became business partners and went into a lumber deal together...on which Pon lost a lot of money. But the money was nothing. The important thing was he had come from China with nothing and rose to be a friend and business partner of a great man like H.H. Carry.

Tragedy came in 1935. His son, the only child, died of blood poisoning from a razor cut. Devastated, Pon Yen adopted two young Chinese boys, and because he was older than most fathers, they called him "Grandfather." The boys were fine, but Pon thought it would be nice to have a little girl around the house. For a time he was "Grandfather" to a girl who was hard to place for adoption. Mixed race was a cruel handicap in Alberta at that time. She was Chinese and Caucasian, though so blonde and fair-skinned that she could appear white. She was with Pon Yen for two happy years, for both, while Charlie Hill, the provincial child welfare chief, sought a home in some cosmopolitan area of the United States where this would not be a problem. She left with her adoptive parents when she was eight. Pon was advised that it was better for her if he didn't try to maintain contact. He accepted the advice but never forgot her or gave up imagining what her life had become. And when time brought him to the age of eighty-six, he learned that she had not forgotten *him*.

On a day in 1959, a white Cadillac made its way through the mountains of British Columbia. The driver was a concert pianist, in the Cadillac class. She had played an engagement in Vancouver and was on a mission. The next day, Pon Yen was looking out the window of his modest home and saw the white Cadillac. It was moving slowly along the street, so slowly that he recognized the California license plate. It was stopping in front of his house. A blonde woman, about thirty and very stylish, was getting out. She was coming up the walk. Pon opened the door. She was saying: "Hello, Grandfather."

32

Dinny McGuire's
IRISHERS

"HAS ANYBODY HERE SEEN KELLY?" It was a popular song in 1909. In Edmonton that year, anybody who went to a ball game would have seen Kelly—at first base. And not only Kelly at first but Grady on the mound and Brennan at third and O'Brien at shortstop and Moran in left field and Shea in centrefield and McGuire at second base. 'Twas himself, Dinny McGuire, the manager. The official name of the team was the Edmonton Eskimos, but wherever they travelled, through towns in the Western Canada Baseball League, they were known as the Edmonton Irishmen, Dinny McGuire's Irishmen, or Dinny McGuire's Irishers. Whether they played the Calgary Cow-Punchers, Lethbridge Miners, Medicine Hat Mad Hatters, Moose Jaw Millers, Regina Bone Pilers, Brandon Angels, or Winnipeg Maroons, they were the Irishmen.

At home, Dinny's gang played on "the ould sod" of Diamond Park, at the foot of McDougall Hill. They may well have been the finest team of Irishmen ever assembled but not, alas, the best team of ball players. Some might argue that Dinny's Irishers illustrate Durocher's Law. It was hard-nosed major league manager Leo Durocher who said, "Nice guys finish last!"

The press was watching all that sorry summer while Dinny's crowd threw games away with spendthrift abandon. The *Bulletin* maintained professional detachment but the *Journal* took their failures as an affront. "McGuire's Irishmen a western disgrace. Somebody should get an injunction to stop these people from representing Edmonton." Sub-headlines told an unchanging story:

Those Irishmen drop another.

Merciful heaven, will they ever win a game?

Irishmen give another exhibition of what is purported to be baseball. Fans of a sympathetic nature asked not to read this account.

(After losing 9–4 to Medicine Hat):
For listless batting and wooden-headed fielding the Irishmen had it over the Hatters. A manager with brains wouldn't do any harm.

A description of the game would be too painful. The appended box score is the most charitable record of events.

The fans in attendance repaired afterwards to the bar of the Edmonton Hotel where the interment of their sorrows took place. (Donald Ross's pioneer hotel was across the street.)

Irish show class. As usual they lose but only by 3 to 2.

When the club went on the road the *Journal*'s indignation travelled with them.

The same old story, at home or abroad, Calgary wins 4 to 2.

The same yesterday, today and forever. Edmonton loses to Cow-Punchers.

Medicine Hat has no trouble making Irish look foolish.

Regina fans see worst yet.

(At Brandon): Agonizing display by Dinny's Irishmen with incidents too painful to mention.

Under this dreary burden of press clippings, McGuire and company slunk into Edmonton for a home stand to end the season. It was August the thirteenth—Friday the thirteenth—a seeming omen of more bad things to come at Diamond Park. But the Irishmen turned the curse upside down. They suddenly started winning. They caught the enthusiasm of the fans— and the *Journal* off guard. Unprepared for competence, the *Journal* turned to ponderous condescending wit. "The Irish didn't commit a single error. They must have learned the art at night school."

Dinny's Irishers could laugh at this laboured jest. They could laugh at anything. They were winning—ball games and fans. And they had a goal: to escape the cellar they had occupied all summer. As thousands cheered, their surge carried them almost into seventh place. Almost. They didn't make it of course. Irish tradition required that. For would Mighty Casey be immortal if he hadn't struck out?

33

THE

Political Insider's
TALE

WHEN STAN FREEMAN LEFT EDMONTON for California, his departure attracted little notice. But to E.E. Owen—the Political Insider—it signalled the end of an era. Freeman was the man with the jaunty motto: "Give me enough money and I'll win any election." He heard whispers that there might be an investigation of one of his efforts in the provincial campaign of 1925. The whispers told him that fun and games had gone out of Alberta politics. Elections had become irretrievably honest. California, here I come!

It was inevitable that Stan Freeman would be known to Eldwin Everett Owen, who went always by his initials E.E. From the time he arrived in Edmonton in 1903, E.E. was inside the wonderland of political intrigue...in addition to many years as a steam engineer and twenty-five as an inspector for the Workmen's Compensation Board. On a grey afternoon in 1958, at his home in Norwood, E.E. provided insights for a lively broadcast on CJCA.

E.E. arrived just too late for a legendary show of election management, in which Lambert and Maloney vied to represent St. Albert in the territorial assembly of the Northwest Territories. The fortunes of politics had given Maloney the Liberal an edge; his crowd was in charge of setting up the polling stations. Confronted with the fact that Lambert's strength was centred around Legal, Maloney's people put the poll as far from Legal as possible—in the bush beyond Pickardville. There were no buildings in those woods, so they set up a tent well off the beaten trail. Then they took down the bridges. The trail crossed several creeks on spans of logs. They took them apart and piled the logs neatly on the far side.

An aerial view of the Royal Alexandra Hospital on 111 Avenue,
with the Edmonton Airport in the background, c. 1930.

Tony Cashman

But supporters of Lambert the Conservative were equal to the challenge. On a day that might have lived in infamy, they made up a convoy of wagons and headed northwest, fording the creeks and beating their way right to the isolated tent. Lambert's people made a full day of it. They stayed to make sure the returning officer counted the votes honestly and made sure he reported them honestly too. Maloney won and thanks to the Lambert crowd, he could claim that the result was honest.

In 1905 the Dominion of Canada "erected" the Province of Alberta, a land of sudden opportunity for people of varied talents and ambitions, including those of Stan Freeman. He allied himself with the ruling party—there was little profit in any other—and the partnership served both well.

E. E. Owen enjoyed a soft chuckle about Freeman's drugstore—on 101 Street where northbound buses now let off customers for Edmonton Centre. It was there in the years 1916 to 1923, when Alberta made its attempt at prohibition. Liquor was sold only in certain drugstores, when prescribed by a doctor for medicinal purposes—an arrangement that ensured great flexibility, with the benefit of the doubt going to the consumer. The punch line to this tale: Freeman's drugstore was owned by the attorney general.

The key to successful election management was control of the voters list. Eventually the province installed a two-party system of enumeration, but in the days of real sport, the people in power appointed the enumerators. As E. E. Owen observed, this one-party mode worked two ways—both to the advantage of the government. A loyal party man could leave obvious supporters of the opposition off the list and add names of fictitious voters. Fictitious voters could be counted on to turn up on election day. The boarding-house districts east of downtown were good places to pad a list. If Freeman's enumerator found a house with eight men qualified to vote, in the spirit of "now is the time for all good men to come to the aid of the party," he might add nine more. When the voters list was published, it was up to the opposition to prove that only eight men were living there. To keep honesty from getting out of hand, Stan Freeman had another trick up his sleeve: infiltrators in the enemy camp.

Someone had to put up the money for elections. E. E. Owen revealed that saloonkeepers bore a heavy, unwilling burden. Before prohibition, a bar owner had to contribute to everybody so that no matter who got in, his license would be secure. He would hear a lot of political talk from the other side of the long, polished bar, and might know where every real vote was going, but there was no predicting the fakes. The public seemed to accept the system as the natural order of things. There was little complaint, though an angry man did write to the editor of the *Bulletin* to let him know a Conservative candidate had offered him a five-dollar bribe. (About what you'd expect from a Conservative, a *Bulletin* subscriber would think.) He wasn't writing to expose the rotter for offering the bribe, but rather for not paying off.

St. Albert continued to provide entertainment, with a feud inside the Liberal Party. Lucien Boudreau was in a contest with his brother-in-law Omer St. Germain over who was the big man in St. Albert. Boudreau had the advantage of being a member of the Alberta Legislature. St. Germain had the advantage of his own newspaper, *Le Progrès* of Morinville.

As the election campaign of 1910 approached, St. Germain's paper was giving his brother-in-law (and his chief, Premier Rutherford) such a drubbing, that Boudreau felt he must go to Morinville and make a speech. He gave St. Germain so much tit-for-tat that when the speech ended, a brawl broke out. Boudreau challenged a heckler, Alphonse Nantel, to a round of fisticuffs. Alphonse declined the offer but published an open letter in the next issue of *Le Progrès*: "Ha, Boudreau, you should not come to our beautiful Morinville and speak your lies and make the big riot. But ha ha, one of your lieutenants has on his face the marks of our beautiful Morinville sidewalk as a souvenir."

Boudreau came out "the big man" from that election. With the next one approaching, there emerged a classic tale from the E. E. Owen collection, which people felt compelled to tell in dialect.

> A Boudreau lieutenant comes with news that St. Germain is
> cruising the backroads handing out five-dollar gold pieces.
> "So, Boudreau, what you gonna do about dat, hey?"
> The big man rubs his ear and says: "You wait and see."
> He sets out on the trail of his brother-in-law.
> Coming into a farmyard he greets the landholder: "Hey,
> Jean-Marcel. St. Germain give you fi'dollar gol'*piece*?"
> "Yeah, fi'dollar gol'*piece*."
> "Ha, dat cheap*skate*. You gimme dat fi'dollar gol'*piece*. I give
> you ten-dollar gol'*piece*."

The next election confirmed Boudreau's status as "big man," though he stood slightly above five feet and was known as "The Little Napoleon of St. Albert." How many women residing on Boudreau Drive know their street preserves the name of the only man to vote against woman suffrage when the historic motion came before the Alberta Legislature in 1916? Boudreau deserves full marks for courage. With Emily Murphy and Nellie McClung looking down from the gallery, he made a last stand, casting the only "nay." And as Mr. Speaker announced the result to a cheering assembly, Boudreau could be heard warning: "You'll be sorry!"

Not all brothers-in-law got along like Boudreau and St. Germain. In Vegreville a returning officer declared his relative elected by acclamation because the opponent spelled his name two ways. On campaign posters, it ended with an S; on the ballots, it ended with a Z.

There were opportunities for returning officers in election management. E. E. Owen laughed about a riding north of Edmonton in which a large area had not yet been opened for settlement. The returning officer created a voters list out of the optimistic air which permeated the new province. On the morning of poll day, a deputy rode off into the woods with the voters list and returned at evening with a box of ballots. The government candidate took that poll by a landslide.

Election management could be overdone. That was Baldy Robb's downfall. His standing with the Liberal Party made him the returning officer at Edson. His candidate there won so handsomely that the opposition got suspicious. They noted that more votes had been cast in a single poll than there were eligible voters in the entire riding. The Alberta Provincial Police found this statistic interesting too and impounded the ballot boxes. The next day Baldy's friends came around to cheer him up. Said one: "Looks pretty bad, I guess." Baldy's reply was an instant classic: "Oh, I don't know. The election's not decided yet. If the Conservatives get in, I'll go to jail, but if the Liberals get in, I'll go to the Senate." The Liberals won, but Baldy lost. He went to jail after all.

The election map of 1921 showed the dramatic growth of Alberta in its sixteen years as a province. The population had gone up from 185,412 to 588,454. Voters would send sixty-one members to the Alberta Legislature instead of twenty-five. Growth in the agricultural and industrial sectors had brought two new parties into play—the United Farmers of Alberta (UFA) and the Dominion Labour Party. The newcomers moved to cooperate in evicting the Liberals from power. E.E. Owen helped negotiate an agreement that the Labour Party and the UFA would stay out of each other's key ridings.

Edson was recognized as Labour's domain. Each union local was to send two delegates to a nomination meeting to choose their standard-bearer. The next morning in Edmonton, party workers waited to hear who the Edson candidate was. When they heard that he was vice-president of the Edson UFA, they knew skulduggery was afoot. They went steaming up to Edson to find out how this betrayal had been accomplished. They learned that the UFA had invented unions out of thin air, each with two delegates, who nominated their vice-president to carry Labour's banner into the election. A new political age based on trust was scuttled by old-style dirty tricks.

The villains were foiled. An honest meeting of genuine unions chose Chris Pattison. Chris took his seat in the fourth Alberta Legislature among three other Labour members, four independents, thirty-eight United Farmers, and fifteen disgruntled Liberals who have been out of power ever since.

Though the next provincial campaign convinced Stan Freeman that fixing elections was no longer a marketable skill in Alberta, the techniques were to serve a good cause in Edmonton—in aid of the Royal Alexandra Hospital. This institution had opened its doors in a burst of civic joie-de-vivre but had fallen on troubled times. The hospital may well be the only hospital anywhere to open with a parade. May 7, 1912 was proclaimed moving day. There were brightly-decorated drays. Carriages and automobiles transported twenty-five patients and all the equipment from the Edmonton General Hospital on Boyle Street (103-A Avenue, east of 97 Street) to 111 Avenue at 102 Street, a site commemorated by the Glenrose. It was a fun parade. Spectators laughed at a single bed riding high on its own festooned dray. Bishop H.A. Gray marshalled sixteen Boy Scouts to help manage the occasion.

Many ordinary citizens wanted to be involved in the hospital. It was a good thing at the time but over twenty years, times changed and it became a problem. The Royal Alex was run by an association like that of the Exhibition. Any citizen could buy a membership and vote for the board of fifteen directors. At the beginning, all were elected but each time the board went to city hall for money, the city claimed more seats, till eventually eight members were appointed by the city. In theory, eight is a controlling majority. But E.E. and friends observed that if seven elected members voted as a block, they could always get one vote from the other side and continue to run the show. By the 1930s, this system was subjecting the Royal Alex to interference by crackpots, well-meaning busybodies, and bleak bean-counters.

Unrest was constant as every year brought an election and a potential new cast of characters. One year, the Civic Government Association got control of the board. They raised the rates for hospital patients and reduced the salaries of the student nurses.

Gouging patients was bad enough but picking on young nurses was too much for E.E. Owen's crowd. They pulled out a proven tactic from their old bag of political tricks. The Civic Government Association didn't suspect anything till late on the final day for new memberships. When the plotters walked in with 150, it was too late for a counterattack. The new members elected seven directors pledged to abolish the association and hand the hospital over to the city of Edmonton. City authorities were more than willing to take over; the province was happy. In 1935, as its last official act, the Hospital Association voted itself out of existence.

Giving the last word to the Political Insider: "It took politics to take politics out of the Royal Alex."

STANDING ON
Guard
FOR THE
ARENA

THERE WAS TO BE A BIG SHOW on February 21, 1982. Those wishing to record it on film understood that they must bring a high-speed camera to catch the moment when the walls came tumbling down. After seven decades, the Edmonton Gardens was to go into history like the Tegler Building and the Marshall Wells Building—an instant brick pile.

"Gardens" was a misnomer, applied halfway through its career, displacing "Arena," an ancient Roman word for "a place where contests and other spectacles were held." This Arena held many spirited contests—hockey at all levels; women's basketball at top level as the world-champion Commercial Grads turned back all challengers; and contests among breeders of prize Percherons. In fact, the building was designed as a showplace for prize animals being bred in the Edmonton countryside. It became a hockey rink on Christmas Day 1913, a happening echoed in Calgary, Regina, Saskatoon, and other prairie centres where the new livestock pavilion offered a ready-made arena: a floor the size and shape for hockey, and seats for 5,000 fans and more. Our Arena served "The Good Old Hockey Game" right up to the coming of the Oilers. In 1942, when I volunteered to stand on guard for Canada in the uniform of the Royal Canadian Air Force, the first thing I stood on guard for was the Arena.

In my dad's war, the Exhibition Grounds were taken over by the army, and soldiers practised digging trenches in the racetrack infield. In the Second World War, the Air Force took temporary possession, and horse barns were again converted to barracks—to process Canadian airmen and receive lads coming from overseas to learn to fly in the Commonwealth Air Training Plan. In the Arena by day, the floor and the seats were centres of ground training. Space under the stands was partitioned for offices. For a half dozen nights, I had it all to myself, armed with a Ross rifle which hadn't been fired since my dad's war and had no ammunition anyway. The authorities had to give us something to do while we waited to go out to training schools, and guard duty was better than the kitchens. The man in the Arena was essentially a fire piquet, there to ring the alarm bells if necessary. But guards at all locations on the grounds—including the fences—were made aware of saboteurs. Saboteurs sank ships and blew up bridges. Gaudy coloured comic strips the size of posters showed what to watch for. A saboteur had a lean and hungry look like "yon Cassius" in the high school production of *Julius Caesar*; his hat was pulled low over his shifty eyes, and there was menace in his twisted smile.

As the midnight hour approached, guards paraded about the grounds and "broke off" at our appointed stations. On certain nights, I'd have the opportunity to research innovative ways of putting in five hours in the solitary expanse of the Arena. To begin, there were a lot of doorknobs under the stands, knobs to be rattled to ensure that the offices were locked and their official contents secure. Knobs were good for about three circuits of the building. Then there was reading material hung on spikes. There were notices of proceedings of the Hogbreeders Association, as the Exhibition Association retained a tiny corner. But the Air Force provided the most notices. Fire Orders. Administrative Orders. Station Standing Orders. Daily Routine Orders were piled one on top of the other, mostly comings-and-goings of recruits—many of which had a cautionary tale about a court-martial in New Brunswick in which Sergeant-Pilot So-and-So was awarded six months detention for taxiing his Harvard aircraft in a reckless and dangerous manner. When those entertainments palled, I could go up into the stands and take a seat—there were five thousand to choose from—and feel the sounds of silence. This expression predates Simon and Garfunkel—it's in the Bible (Book of Kings, story of Elijah)—and none describes better the vibrations in a vast empty barn that has rocked with emotions of basketball and hockey crowds.

In the twenty-first century, Edmonton plays hockey in a league with Calgary, Montreal, and New York. In the 1930s and earliest 1940s, Edmonton played in leagues with Calgary, Olds, and Ponoka. Players were local amateurs. Teams were sponsored by local firms, notably Gainer's packing plant and Dominion Motors for reasons of business and civic responsibility.

In the twenty-first century, Edmonton offers hockey players millions of dollars to come here. One year in the late 1930s, the Exhibition Board sponsored a hockey team called the Eskimos, which was so bad that the next year they changed the name to the Flyers and sought to lure a coach from Ontario—a player-coach for reasons of dollars. Their choice was a centre named Eddie O'Keefe. Most players skated faster than O'Keefe, but few could think as fast. Eddie thought the additional offer of a job driving a streetcar was one no reasonable man could dismiss.

The wily O'Keefe did not come as a man for all seasons. Hockey was confined to winter because artificial ice was not universal. A curling bonspiel usually brought on a January thaw; in hockey playoffs, a sign of spring could be wood shavings poking through the frost.

In the twenty-first century, there are four officials on the ice: two referees and two linesmen. In the 1930s, we also had four: a referee, a linesman, and the two goal judges, who stood behind the nets in their mufflers and overcoats and shot their right arms in the air to signal that a puck had gone in. They held their arms high till the tumult subsided. More dramatic by far than the impersonal red light and raging bullhorn.

While senior teams—and one professional crew—came and went, the juniors were a constant. The South Side Athletic Club was maintained by taxi-man Jimmy Smith, unofficial "mayor" of Old Strathcona. The Maple Leafs were based on the Alberta Avenue Community Rink. The EACs (Edmonton Athletic Club) were at the 119 Street rink.

Senior teams couldn't charge admission on Sundays. So Sunday afternoons at the Arena were left to the juniors and their fans. Here, a matter of perception should be noted. To adults looking down kindly from above, junior players appeared to be kids. But looking up from sub-teen level, they were titans, easy to recognize on the ice or on the street. Hockey players wore little padding anywhere and none on their heads. Transportation to and from the Arena was affordable with streetcar tickets two for a nickel. On Sundays, admission had to be by "free-will donation." Team sponsors knew paper money was a vain hope, and the term "silver collection" was a hint that coins should be silver. But they got a lot of nickel and copper and often not even that as kids sailed through calling out: "Social Credit." When a brash kid invoked Mr. Aberhart's economic vision to include free hockey, the scowling gatekeeper couldn't argue.

We liked to watch Sunday heroics from the south end, brother John and I and Ed and Jack and Albert, an unpromising collection of humanity if ever there was one. We liked the tenth row, of which there were fourteen. While sitting on guard for the Arena, I counted rows, upstairs-downstairs, section by section around the building. After revisiting our Sunday spot, I'd move to other vantage points where fragments of hockey games hung in dust churned up from wood shavings on the floor. Though I wasn't there for "the most exciting goal ever scored in Edmonton," I saw "the most exciting defensive play."

The most exciting goal was scored in March 1923. I wasn't born until April that year, but the goal was described so often and so vividly by Uncle Raoul Gaboury, the ultimate fan, that I could go to the spot where he'd watched with cousin Paul, age eight, on his knee. What made this goal the most exciting? It put Edmonton into the Stanley Cup final. The Eskimos (our hockey teams were also Eskimos then) were locked in a semi-final series with the Regina Capitals—two games, total points. Edmonton carried a 2–1 lead into the second game, and fan confidence soared as it went quickly to 3–1. But in the third period, Regina was coming back. Dick Irvine scored. Barney Stanley scored. At the end of regulation, the teams stood even at 3–all. The prospect of overtime was so stressful that a man nearby feared a heart attack. He went down to pace below the stands, like an expectant father, hearing all the emotions a hockey crowd can express—dismay, relief, disbelief, "referee rage." But at 10:25 of overtime, the referee proved competent after all. He awarded a penalty shot to Edmonton. Everyone in the rink knew Duke Keats would take it. In dead silence, the crowd saw Duke skate

A new front grafted onto an old barn transforms the Arena into the Gardens and makes a program cover for the Allan Cup Flyers and defenceman Gordie Watt.

Tony Cashman

to the puck, his head went down, the puck flew, the arm of the goal judge was in the air and Edmonton was in the Stanley Cup final with the Ottawa Senators. Ottawa won, a sad story. Even sadder, shortly after, the NHL moved the entire Western Hockey League to American cities, and Edmonton would wait sixty years for another chance.

The most exciting goal was a high-speed moment. The most exciting defensive play, on the other hand, was in aching slow motion through a minute-and-a-half of anxiety. Making my rounds in the Arena, I'd move from where Uncle Raoul saw "Duke Keats score the winning goal in overtime" to where I saw "Foley rag the puck." It was a long climb to the bleachers in the north end, perched on top of the big door designed as a grand entry for prize livestock. Seats were not reserved or even marked. Capacity was a matter of how many could squeeze on. Foley ragged the puck at a critical stage of a crucial contest as the Edmonton Athletic Club juniors battled the St. Boniface Seals in the western playoff of 1939.

Penalties put the EACs two men down. The situation seemed to threaten memorable offense, but the opposite happened. The EACs sent out a secret weapon: Bud Foley grabbed the puck at the faceoff and took it on a slow ramble, up and down and across the ice, herding it like a prize hen, spinning away from all would-be takers. As he moved in our direction, his slow smile seemed to say: "Shucks, this is nothing." A cheer grew in unbroken crescendo. When he went off, passing the puck to a teammate, the ovation rattled the boards under my feet.

In the twenty-first century, hundred-dollar sticks break dramatically and often. Back then, when a two-dollar wooden model fractured, it was an event. Destiny put me in the right place in a box along the rink boards—the night Louie Holmes broke his. As play went on, the referee scooped up the remains and conferred them on me. Louie had played in the NHL, so the broken stick had a certain mystique. With a couple of nails, black tape, and a few inches off the top, it worked just fine.

The referee himself was a story. He didn't have a whistle. He carried a school bell, and when an infraction occurred, clang-clang-clang went the bell, like the one on the trolley in *Meet Me in St. Louis*. The referee was a lawyer in the Tegler Building, and went on to be president of the National Hockey League. His name? Clarence Campbell.

As we stood on guard for the Exhibition Grounds, we lived in daily hope of going out to a flying school to guard airplanes. Perhaps one in fifty of the chaps so keen to fly had ever been inside an airplane. Aviation was the Great Adventure of the twentieth century and was suddenly open to any youth with eighteen years, 20–20 vision, and grade twelve. Eventually we moved out. I flew over Germany, and the Arena survived the war untouched by sabotage. And many years would pass before it was demonstrated that a saboteur wouldn't have had much luck anyhow.

The Commercial Grads didn't return after the war, but hockey did. With a new name (the Gardens) and a new front, the old barn was home for the amateur Allan Cup Flyers; the professional Flyers of Poile, Ullman, and Bucyk; the world champion Waterloo Mercurys; the Oil Kings in their first incarnation; and ultimately the Oilers.

In 1974 the Oilers moved across 118 Avenue to the Coliseum. But the Gardens remained useful for many events, until 1982 when its time was declared done. A demolition expert came from Kelowna to make the walls come tumbling down.

The end was scheduled for February 21. Fifty charges of TNT were placed at stress points. Special guests were invited. Police kept spectators with their high-speed cameras three hundred yards away for safety. The button was pushed. Puffs of smoke emerged, but the pigeons were indifferent. The old girl had a surprise for everybody. The walls were lined with steel wire mesh. Four days later, the expert tried again with 250 charges. Doors and windows blew out. The pigeons were impressed, but a terse headline in the *Journal* gave the score: Gardens 2, TNT 0. The Arena had to be wrestled to the ground piece by piece. In going, it put up a contest as spirited as any ever held within its stubborn walls.

Index